T0209930

A *Dramatic Ministry* *for* Small Churches

Plays Written Specifically for Small Churches

HOLLY LANGSTER

WESTBOW
PRESS®
A DIVISION OF THOMAS NELSON
& ZONDERVAN

Copyright © 2018 Holly Langster.

All rights reserved. No part of this book may be used or reproduced by any means, graphic, electronic, or mechanical, including photocopying, recording, taping or by any information storage retrieval system without the written permission of the author except in the case of brief quotations embodied in critical articles and reviews.

Scriptures taken from the Holy Bible, New International Version®, NIV®. Copyright © 1973, 1978, 1984, 2011 by Biblica, Inc.™ Used by permission of Zondervan. All rights reserved worldwide. www.zondervan.com The "NIV" and "New International Version" are trademarks registered in the United States Patent and Trademark Office by Biblica, Inc.

WestBow Press books may be ordered through booksellers or by contacting:

WestBow Press
A Division of Thomas Nelson & Zondervan
1663 Liberty Drive
Bloomington, IN 47403
www.westbowpress.com
1 (866) 928-1240

Because of the dynamic nature of the Internet, any web addresses or links contained in this book may have changed since publication and may no longer be valid. The views expressed in this work are solely those of the author and do not necessarily reflect the views of the publisher, and the publisher hereby disclaims any responsibility for them.

Any people depicted in stock imagery provided by Getty Images are models, and such images are being used for illustrative purposes only. Certain stock imagery © Getty Images.

ISBN: 978-1-9736-3980-0 (sc)
ISBN: 978-1-9736-3979-4 (hc)
ISBN: 978-1-9736-3981-7 (e)

Library of Congress Control Number: 2018910979

Print information available on the last page.

WestBow Press rev. date: 9/27/2018

Introduction

It is so challenging for small churches to have a positive presence in the communities where they reside. Let's face it, community service is an expensive and time-consuming venture, and sometimes, it can feel as though the same small group of people give and give. While God expects us to care for others and help those in need, He has also asked us to spread the gospel. For small churches whose expense budgets are paper thin, it's really important to find creative ways to serve the community and spread the gospel. I come from a small church in a small community. I have attended this church for almost fifteen years. Heber Springs, Arkansas, has a population of 7,301 people. There are an abundance of churches in Heber Springs, but many of them are small. A handful of them are large enough to have a bus for bringing kids to Sunday school or a daycare to support young families, but most have nothing more than weekly Sunday school and church services, with Wednesday night Bible studies.

This left our church wondering what we could do. What might make us stand out and be a church that families would like to attend? As the mother of a young son, I was desperate to find a way to attract kids to our church. The only kids present on Sundays were the ones I picked up on my way in: my son's friends who otherwise didn't go to church. In order to keep them interested in attending, I began holding children's church during the preaching service. They would attend Sunday school; join the adults in the sanctuary for music, announcements, and any special presentations held that day; and then we would go to separate building for a lesson and activity focused at their learning level and interests. I quickly learned that the more activity involved in our Sunday lessons, the better the children would engage in the lesson of the day.

My son always loved to wear costumes, and I discovered that most of his friends did too. With this information, and my desire to keep the kids interested, we began to practice reciting elements of the Christmas story or the Easter story to perform for the church on those special Sundays. The kids would dress up like nativity characters or wear their Easter Sunday morning best and really get excited about their roles in the service. The kids loved getting the opportunity to get on the stage and be a part of the church service. With this successful venture underfoot, I decided to try to find some skits they could perform on Sunday mornings that might show what they learned in children's church, get them used to speaking in front of people (an important life skill), and perhaps even draw in the families of the kids who would be performing that particular day. With this, a ministry was born.

Our church has grown, but we're still small. Our claim to fame in our community, however, is our annual Christmas play. We pack the building, and the community looks forward to coming to see what the people of Heber Springs Calvary Missionary Baptist Church have come up with each year.

This book is a collection of some of the plays written for the kids (and the adults) of the church. As the church has grown, the plays have grown. We have found that people love to get involved by building sets, painting, making costumes, running the lights and sound, coordinating props, performing music, and of course, playing characters on stage. Everyone has an opportunity to get involved. Not all of the plays included here are Christmas plays, but most are. I hope you enjoy them and find use for them in your church as you begin to develop a dramatic ministry in your own community.

Christmas Holiday

Cast

Lucas: a young boy

Hannah: a young girl

Dayton: a young boy

Loretta: a man or a woman who represents the matriarch or patriarch of a family

Innkeeper: male or female

Mary: a female

Joseph: a male

Angel: male or female

Wise Man: any age

Shepherd: any age

Baby Jesus: can be a doll if needed

Timekeeper: anyone, or use a projection of a clock on a screen if you use screens for song lyrics

You can add or take away characters as you have people to fill roles, and the costumes can be flexible. Use a candy cane, an ornament, and a wrapped present, or any other combination of Christmas costumes your kids can imagine. Remember that part of the fun is having some say in the costumes.

The People of Bethlehem

Three kids walk to the front door of a home
dressed in Christmas-themed costumes.

Hannah Ames, Lucas Langster and Dayton Wall
in Holiday Christmas

LUCAS. Are you sure this is a good idea, Hannah?

HANNAH. Yes. I'm telling you, this is brilliant.

LUCAS. What do people say when you knock on their doors and say, "Trick or treat," at Christmas?

HANNAH. So far, they've been pretty okay with it. I've gotten some candy canes, some apples, and Miss Frances gave me money. Come on. I'll knock, and you guys help me yell, "Trick or treat!" You in, Lucas?

LUCAS. I guess so.

HANNAH. You in, Dayton?

DAYTON. I'm in.

> Hannah knocks on the door; Loretta answers.

LORETTA. Well, hi, kids.

HANNAH, LUCAS, and DAYTON. Trick or treat!

LORETTA. What?

DAYTON. We said, "Trick or treat."

LORETTA. I think you've got your holidays mixed up.

HANNAH. No, I think we should be able to go trick-or-treating on all holidays. I even went on Thanksgiving.

LORETTA. What did you get on Thanksgiving when you went trick-or-treating?

HANNAH. I got some turkey and a baked sweet potato.

LORETTA, *looking around the area.* Am I on *Candid Camera*?

LUCAS. What's *Candid Camera*?

LORETTA. I just can't believe you're out trick-or-treating on Christmas. Didn't you get gifts today?

DAYTON, *showing her a truck.* Yes, I got this truck. I really like it.

HANNAH. We did, but we're out to see what else we can get—

LUCAS and DAYTON, *interrupting.* By trick-or-treating.

LORETTA, *after pausing to think.* Do you know what Christmas is all about?

DAYTON. Yes, we know what Christmas is about.

HANNAH. Santa Claus brings presents, and the family eats dinner for lunch.

LUCAS. And then Mom kicks us out of the house because she's mad that she has to clean the kitchen up all by herself while everyone else naps and plays with presents.

LORETTA. I see. I think maybe, just maybe, I have a little something for you. Wait right here.

Loretta goes inside.

DAYTON, *excitedly*. What is she gonna do?

LUCAS. I bet she is bringing us homemade Christmas candy.

HANNAH. Yeah, fudge … cookies. Maybe even pie.

> The kids stand quiet for just a minute. Someone walks by with a huge clock. (If possible, use one that allows you to spin the hands at a rapid pace to indicate the passing of a lot of time.) The kids sit down on the stage as though they have been waiting for hours and just cannot physically stand a moment longer.

DAYTON. How much longer?

HANNAH. I'm so tired. We should go to other houses.

LUCAS. I'm bored. This lady is crazy.

The huge clock walks by again, and then Loretta returns to the door.

LORETTA. Okay, kids, my family and I are going to tell you a story. When the story is over, we will give you something nice for your trick-or-treat bags. Okay?

KIDS. Okay!

> They walk to the living-room set at stage left and sit on the floor around her as she reads the Christmas story from her rocking chair. Loretta's family is dressed in Bethlehem attire, ready to act out the story as she reads it aloud.

LORETTA. We want to tell you the story of Christmas. Over two thousand years ago, on this earth lived two people, Mary and Joseph. They were engaged to be married, and they were very much in love. God knew they were good people and would be good parents. Because they had loved God all their lives, He chose them to be the earthly parents of His only Son, Jesus.

God sent an angel to the home of Mary to tell her she had been chosen to be the mother of Jesus, the Savior, the Messiah God had promised His people. Now Mary was scared. She was very young and not yet married. She had to explain all of this to Joseph and trust that he would understand. He did. And with God's help, they managed to get through the pregnancy and travel safety to Bethlehem before Jesus was born. But when they got to Bethlehem, they quickly came to the realization that it was time for Jesus to be born.

> Lights up on Mary and Joseph, walking in from the kitchen hall, stage right.

MARY. Oh, Joseph, I just don't think I can make it much farther. We must find a place to stop.

JOSEPH. I know, Mary, and I'm so sorry this has been such a hard trip. Let's get a room here for the night and get some rest.

> He knocks on the door, and the innkeeper answers.

JOSEPH. Sir, my wife and I have traveled a long way, and we need a room for the night. Can you—

INNKEEPER, *interrupting.* No. There is no room in the inn.

JOSEPH. Please, sir, do you have anywhere we can stay? My wife is so tired.

INNKEEPER. Well, I suppose I could let you stay out in the barn.

JOSEPH. Anywhere, sir. We'll take a room anywhere we can get one.

INNKEEPER. All right, come on. (*The innkeeper comes out as the lights come up center stage. He walks the couple to center stage, outside of the barn.*) This is the barn. You're welcome to stay in here.

JOSEPH. Thank you, sir.

MARY. Thank you.

LORETTA. Well, that night it happened; the baby Jesus was born. While He was being born, God put a huge star in the sky so that people who were awaiting the arrival of the Savior could come and see Him. Some of the visitors included shepherds and wise men. Angels stood guard over the newborn King. Even the animals in the barn worshipped Him.

An angel, wise man, and shepherd come and join the nativity scene. (Option: A wise man steps up to center stage when Loretta starts the verbiage above. He stops at center stage and begins to sing "Do You Hear What I Hear?" When finished, he stands at the manger scene.)

LORETTA. Everyone who came to see the baby brought gifts. See, Mary and Joseph were going to have to leave soon because the king of the country ordered all babies be killed. He obviously did not know God. The gifts that came to baby Jesus that day were not typical baby gifts, like toys and blankets and cute clothes. They were quite valuable. God knew the young family would need money to move and survive. God always takes care of those who trust Him. Some gifts were not of great monetary value, but they were gifts of great love.

> Option: A shepherd walks up with drum singing "The Little Drummer Boy." When finished, he stands at the manger scene.

LORETTA. God had promised the people of the world a Savior, the Messiah. He was to come to earth and live among us, experiencing what we experience and feeling what we feel, so we can know He truly understands everything we're going through. He was also sent here to die for our sins so that we would never again have to offer sacrifices or go through a priest to talk to God like they had to do in Old Testament times. Because of Jesus, we have a direct link to the throne of God through Jesus Christ.

Jesus being born here on earth was a really great gift. He lived as a man for thirty-three years and then was killed as the ultimate sacrifice for our sins. Because of Jesus, we have the opportunity to live forever and ever in heaven with God.

> Option: Mary sings "Hallelujah—Light Has Come" with angels harmonizing.

LUCAS. I didn't know all of that about Jesus.

HANNAH. I didn't know all of that about Christmas.

> Dayton walks over, leaves his truck in front on the manger, and kneels in front of the baby.

LORETTA. Dayton, what are you doing?

DAYTON. This is my gift for baby Jesus. He should have a toy.

KIDS, *after walking over and leaving their trick-or-treat bags in front of the manger with Dayton's truck and kneeling beside Jesus.* Yes, He should get Christmas gifts. It's His birthday.

Loretta hugs the kids, and they all sing one verse *of* "Away in a Manger" and then "Joy to the World."

Lights down. The end.

The Tiger, the Turtle, and the Snake

As I mentioned, these kids loved to wear costumes. This is a short Sunday morning skit written specifically for the costumes they chose to wear. I put the title of the play on the projector screen and in the bulletin that morning to help ensure everyone knew what each character was, even though our costumes were superb.

Cast

TIGER: child

TURTLE: child

SNAKE: child

Lights up with Turtle on stage. He stretches and yawns and slowly walks (crawls) across the stage. Suddenly, Tiger comes bounding up the center aisle, and when she sees Turtle, she starts to attack. Turtle sees her coming and pulls into his shell.

Tiger. Come out of there, Turtle! I'm hungry, and I want to eat you for lunch.

Tiger circles the Turtle and tries to get him to come out.

Tiger. Come on, Turtle; come out of that shell. I've been looking for food all morning. I'm hungry.

Turtle. Go away, Tiger! I'm no good to eat; go eat something else!

Tiger. No! I'm eating you; there is nothing else to eat.

Tiger sits next to Turtle and waits for him to come out.

Turtle, *praying quietly.* Dear God, please provide this tiger some lunch that isn't me.

Tiger. What did you say?

Turtle. I asked God to provide you some lunch that isn't me. I would like to live. I have a family and friends, and I don't think God is done with me yet on this earth, so I would like for Him to provide you some lunch so I can live.

Tiger. Who is God? Is He in your shell with you?

Turtle. No, He's not in my shell. He's in my heart. God is the creator of the universe and of humans and animals, and He loves us! All He asks is that we love Him too. He is my best friend and my provider. I know He will provide for you too. Why don't you ask Him?

Tiger. I don't see Him to ask.

TURTLE. You don't have to see Him; just know He is there. He's listening, and He wants to help you.

TIGER. What should I say?

TURTLE. Just ask Him for some lunch. I'll ask with you.

TIGER. Uh, okay. God, sir, would you please provide me with some lunch? I'm awfully hungry.

As Tiger sits quietly looking at the sky, as if the food will fall from the heavens, Turtle reluctantly peeks his head out of his shell. A snake walks across the stage with a basket on his "arm."

TURTLE. Hey, there's a snake with a basket.

TIGER. Ah ha! God sent me a big ol' snake to eat; do I like snake?

Tiger prepares to pounce on Snake.

TURTLE, *coming out of his shell*. Wait! That snake has a basket; be a good tiger, and stop trying to eat everyone. Let's go see what's in the basket.

TIGER. Hey, Snake, what's in the basket?

SNAKE. This is a lunch I fixed for my family. I was going to surprise them with a picnic, but they had the same idea, and we ended up with two lunches. I'm taking this one back home.

TURTLE. Well, Snake, Tiger here is hungry, and I haven't had lunch, either. Would you be willing to share?

SNAKE. I would love to share. My family went swimming, and I love to meet new friends.

The three sit down together, and Snake shares his lunch. Snake prepares to take a bite of his sandwich.

Turtle and Tiger, *together.* Thank you, God, for lunch!

Snake, *looking up.* Who's God?

Turtle and Tiger smile to each other.

Lights down.

King Goliath

This is a twisted story that falls somewhere between David and Goliath and King Kong. Kids love it!

Cast

Dave Molt: a young boy

Samantha Marie: a young girl

King Goliath: whoever fits the gorilla costume (We used a boy—he loved being the gorilla.)

Dad: adult or teen male

Stagehand: no specific requirement

Policeman: adult or teen (You can use a child.)

Zookeeper: adult or teen (You can use a child.)

Radio announcer: someone from the soundboard or audience with a microphone

Scene 1

Dave is a cowboy, dressed in jeans, spurs, boots, and Stetson hat. Today he is out in his barn, feeding his cattle. While he is in his barn, he likes to talk to God.

DAVE. God, you're just so good; thank you for this day! I love spending my mornings alone with You while I work on this farm. Thank you for the animals, the land, and the strength to do what I do. I love being your child. Help me to serve you every day by serving others.

While feeding his animals, Dave greets them all and says good morning.

DAVE. Hi, Bessie, girl; how are you this morning? Hey there, Buster! (*Feel free to ad lib, addressing whatever animals you can display on your stage.*)

Scene 2

Samantha Marie is a Broadway actress who is currently very famous. Unfortunately, she knows she's famous and tends to make life a little bit miserable for those around her. Samantha is backstage in her makeup chair, getting ready for the show to start, when her assistant comes in, excited to have the item Samantha requested.

ASSISTANT. Ms. Marie, I brought the eyeshadow you asked for. (*He sets the eyeshadow on her table.*)

SAMANTHA. This isn't what I asked for! I asked for green eyeshadow; this is blue. Get it right.

She slams the eyeshadow down on the table and turns away.

The assistant leaves, looking very sad and beaten down; he comes right back in.

ASSISTANT. Ms. Marie, you're on in five minutes.

SAMANTHA. I hear you. An actress's work is never done.

She walks off toward what would be the front of the stage (the rear of the actual stage).

Scene 3

Back in the barn, Dave is just sweeping up when his dad walks in.

DAD. Did you get those horses fed?

DAVE. Yeah, I got 'em fed.

DAD. I just watched the news, and the craziest thing happened: A gorilla broke out of the zoo and is running wild downtown. I hope they don't have to kill him or anything, but I don't know how to capture a gorilla. The news said that we are supposed to stay off the streets.

Scene 4

SAMANTHA, *taking her bows and blowing kisses (remember, she has her back to the actual audience because the pretend stage is behind her).* Thank you, thank you, everyone, thank you so much.

She walks back into her dressing room, where she is facing the actual audience now.

SAMANTHA. I'm so glad that show is over, and I have the weekend off. I'm just completely exhausted.

She grabs her jacket and leaves.

SAMANTHA. It's going to be a long walk home.

She walks down the center aisle; as she does, King Goliath enters from the other side of the stage and sees Samantha. He follows her; she sees the gorilla and stops, and then starts to move faster. He follows her down the center aisle as she runs off.

Samantha, *screaming.* Help!

Scene 5

Dave is in the barn with his dad, drinking coffee and listening to the news on the radio.

Radio announcer. This just in: an escaped zoo gorilla named "King Goliath" has captured the world-famous Samantha Marie. Ms. Marie was leaving her late-night Broadway show and walking back to her apartment when she was apparently confronted by the gorilla. Some witnesses say they saw her running from the gorilla; others say that she was caught by the gorilla, who threw her over his shoulder. We do not know where she is, but special forces have been deployed.

Dave. The gorilla has Samantha Marie; what are they going to do?

A knock on the door; Dave's dad answers. It's the police.

Police. Hello sir, we're looking for men to come help us defeat a gorilla that has escaped from the zoo. It has knocked out all the special forces teams, and the local police department is out of options. Would you be willing to fight with us?

Dad. Oh man, uh, I'm not a very good shot.

Police. It's okay, sir; we don't think you'll have to shoot; we just need people who can help us serve as distractions and help hold the gorilla down once we get close enough to shoot him with a sleeping dart.

Dad. Uh, sure, uh, you know, I would love to help, and normally I would, but I have this old football injury that's really been acting up, and well,

I'm just not sure that I would be any help. I might be more of a hindrance to you than a help.

DAVE. I'll do it. I'll do it. I'll help you hold down the gorilla.

DAD. No, he's not big enough; no.

DAVE. I can, I can. I know I can.

DAD. No, I don't think so.

DAVE. Just today I killed three coyotes that were trying to attack the cows, and last week I killed a bobcat with my bare hands. I can do it. I can do it.

DAD. I'm sorry, officer. I don't think we should come with you.

POLICE. Okay.

The policeman leaves.

DAD, *walking away.* I better go lock the doors and windows—there's a gorilla on the loose!

As Dad is walking around closing windows and locking them, Dave steps forward and talks to himself (facing the audience).

DAVE. I'm not afraid of a gorilla! (*Grabbing his slingshot, he walks off.*)

DAD, *still talking to himself as he walks out of the other area of the barn.* Don't you think, Dave? That gorilla is brave, capturing someone as famous as Samantha Marie; there's liable to be a worldwide riot, don't you think, Dave? Dave? Dave?"

Looking around and realizing that Dave isn't there, he panics.

DAD, *yelling in desperation and fear.* "David? David?" (*He runs off.*)

Scene 6

King Goliath has Samantha captured, and she is trying to talk to him. They are sitting *on some large rocks at the far corner of the stage.*

SAMANTHA. Can I get a drink? There is water right over there in that stream, and I could sure use a drink.

King Goliath grunts and growls as if to say no.

Samantha tries to move slowly away, and King Goliath lets her know loudly that she is not permitted to move. He jumps off of the rock and gets in front of her. He is facing her with his back to the audience when Dave comes up the center aisle and approaches the gorilla from behind.

Samantha sees Dave walking toward them and shakes her head no at him. King Goliath notices the distraction and looks over, also seeing Dave. King Goliath stands up tall and thumps his chest.

DAVE. You don't scare me, gorilla!

King Goliath tries harder to scare Dave away.

DAVE. I said, you don't scare me, gorilla! I might not be a very big person, but I have a great big God! He made me, and He loves me more than anything in this world. He made you and Ms. Marie too, and He's not gonna let you hurt or kill her. If you think you can just take people, you have another thing coming; you might as well let her go.

King Goliath growls and thumps his chest as Dave pulls back his slingshot and flings a rock that misses King Goliath. King Goliath ducks and is mad that Dave is throwing rocks at him. King Gorilla thumps and growls loudly and charges Dave. Dave slings another rock, and it hits King Goliath in the head as he is running toward Dave. King Goliath falls backward to the ground.

Dave calls for the zookeepers right away as he walks toward Samantha.

DAVE. I've got the gorilla knocked out here on the top of the hill in the park. Come quickly before he awakens, and you can get him back to the zoo. (*Dave makes it over to Samantha.*) Are you okay, Ms. Marie?

SAMANTHA. Yes, I'm fine; thank you so much. You saved my life!

The zookeeper arrives to capture the gorilla.

ZOOKEEPER. Thank you for capturing King Goliath! You're mighty brave.

DAVE. It's not that I'm so brave, ma'am. I've just got a mighty brave God.

Famous Sons of the Bible

This is a great Father's Day Sunday morning skit for kids to do.

Cast

News reporter: any gender or age

Cameraman: any gender or age

Joseph: any age

Isaac: any age

Jesus: any age (it is best if all three "sons" are either adults or children, not a mix)

The news reporter walks out on stage with handheld mic, talking to his cameraman, who carries a camera on his right shoulder and squats to film everything the news reporter does.

NEWS REPORTER. Are you ready? Is this thing on?

He taps the microphone.

CAMERAMAN. Okay, here we go. Five, four, three, two (*he shows the number of fingers in the air on his left hand as he says them. He does not say "one," only shows it with his finger and then points to the news reporter to imply it is time for him to talk*).

NEWS REPORTER. Good evening, this is Justin Newton from Channel 25 KING News. We're here at the gates of heaven this Father's Day morning. We're so excited because we've received special permission to enter into heaven and interview some famous sons of the Bible! Look, the gates are open now; let's go.

They walk into heaven and see a group gathered.

NEWS REPORTER. I see a group gathered here; let's go see who they are. Hello, I'm Justin Newton from Channel 25 KING News; we're here to interview some famous sons of the Bible. Might you be one?

JOSEPH. Yes, I guess I am.

NEWS REPORTER. Great; tell me, sir, what is your name?

JOSEPH. My name is Joe.

NEWS REPORTER. Joe, who is your father?

JOSEPH. My father is Jacob. He's around here somewhere; I'm not sure where.

NEWS REPORTER. Joe, tell me why your father is such a great father.

JOSEPH. Sure, I'd love to. My dad is the best dad ever. He loves me and my mother with all of his heart. He would do anything for us.

NEWS REPORTER. What kind of things did your dad do to show how much he loved you?

JOSEPH. Well, one time he bought me this beautiful coat. It was long and beautiful and had every color you could imagine in it. My dad really loves me; he is a really great guy. My brothers ... not so much!

NEWS REPORTER. I see; well, thank you, Joe, for sharing a story about your father. How about you, sir; are you a famous son of the Bible?

Isaac. Well, I think so. I'm actually *his* (*pointing to Joe*) grandfather! My name is Isaac.

News reporter. That's great! Isaac, tell us something great about your dad this Father's Day.

Isaac. Well, my dad is the only man I know who is listed in the Bible as a friend of God. He worked his whole life to please God.

News reporter. Tell about an experience you remember with your dad.

Isaac. Oh, I can tell you about an experience! One day, Dad said, "Hey Isaac, let's go up on the mountain and worship God." So I put on my shoes and off we went. Do you know what he did when we got there? He tied me down to a stone bench, put firewood underneath me, and raised a knife to slice me open! He was going to sacrifice me!

News reporter. Oh my goodness; what happened?

Isaac. God had to stop him! He put a ram in the thorns and told Dad to get the ram and leave me alone. Whew! That knife was so close to me, it split the hairs on my chest! Dad loves me, but he loves God more; honestly, that's how it should be.

News reporter. Wow! That is a great story! Thank you for sharing! (*Looks at the audience.*) I see one more man over there; let's go get an interview from him, and then we'll go. Excuse me, sir; my name is Justin Newton from Channel 25 KING News. We're here today doing interviews of famous sons of the Bible for Father's Day. Are you a famous son?

Jesus. I am.

Justin. That's great! Could you tell us something about your dad?

Jesus. I can. My Father is kind, loving, honorable, just, and generous. My Father completed the sacrifice of His Son. He did it so that all people could live eternally if they so choose. There is no pain like that of losing a child;

my Father suffered that for you. My Father loves more than any father ever could. My Father is love.

NEWS REPORTER. So you must be …

JESUS. I am.

NEWS REPORTER. There you have it, ladies and gentlemen; the most famous of the famous sons from the Bible. The lesson we've learned today: God so loved the world that He gave His only Son, that whosoever believes in Him should not perish but have everlasting life. Happy Father's Day.

God's Family

God's Family is a story written around the music of the Collingsworth Family. I received their CD as a birthday gift one year, and the music spoke to me in a beautiful way. I was able to write this story around the songs that the adults in our church could perform. The kids served as the kids in the family and had fun dancing as the animals in the song "Not Just Another Rainy Day." We performed this as our Easter play one year. I hope you enjoy it as much as we did.

Cast

Bob: the father of three adult daughters

Liz: his wife, the mother of three adult daughters

Beth: the youngest of the three daughters—not married and unsettled

Michelle: the oldest of the three daughters, married to Steve, mother of Mike and Toby

Steve: married to Michelle, father to Mike and Toby

Mike: son of Michelle and Steve

Toby: son of Michelle and Steve

Stacie: middle daughter of Liz and Bob, wife of Rod, mother of Jack and Lillie

Rod: husband to Stacie and father to Jack and Lillie

Jack: son of Rod and Stacie

Lillie: daughter of Rod and Stacie

Preacher: a silhouette character who has no lines (We had "Rod" do this part too.)

Doctor: male or female

Narrator: male or female (This person needs to be charismatic and a great storyteller.)

God's Family practice

The lights come up on a stage full of people performing a choreographed version of "Joy Unspeakable," sung by the family cast.

Lights down on the cast and a single spotlight up on the narrator.

NARRATOR. Christians, who are these people? From where do they come? Why are they so happy? What gives them this joy unspeakable of which they sing? Is it really Jesus? Can it be that a man who lived on this earth 2,018 years ago can have that much influence over the lives of people who choose to follow Him today? Perhaps it's a cult, this Christianity. Surely not! This joy does seem so real!

How is that Christians came to be? What caused them to go from average human beings, living life as it seemed most normal, to being children of the King? The Bible says that the Son of God came to earth as a baby, grew to be a man, and lived a perfect life, without sin. The amazing thing is that He was tempted to sin in every way. The Bible tells us that He faced those temptations so we could know that He, in His human form, faced the same challenges we face every day. At the age of thirty-three, Jesus died on a cross, but He didn't just close His eyes and die. He was beaten, ridiculed, humiliated, tortured, nailed to a tree, hung in the air, and left to die in agony. This was the perfect, flawless Son of God, the spotless Lamb who died so that our sins might be forgiven and so that we may have eternal life. For God so loved the world that He gave His only begotten Son, that whosoever believes in Him shall have eternal life.

Lights down on the narrator and up on the stage for the song.

"At Calvary" is sung by the family cast.

Lights down on the cast and up on the narrator.

NARRATOR. Maybe bad things never happen to Christian people. Could it be? Could it be that when you devote your life to Jesus, He protects you from bad things ever happening to you again? Maybe that's it! Let's look closer at the lives of these Christian people and see what kinds of things they really do experience.

Scene 1

In the home of Bob and Liz, parents of three daughters and four grandchildren, preparations are being made for five-year-old Lillie's birthday party.

LIZ. Bob, are you finished in the yard?

BOB. Yes, dear.

LIZ. I want the yard to look nice for the party.

BOB, *under his breath*. Even though it's in the kitchen?

LIZ. What did you say, dear?

BOB. Oh, oh, I just said, um, yes, dear.

LIZ. Well, it's not very often that one of our grandchildren wants to have their birthday party at our house. Usually they want to go to Chuckie Cheese or the trampoline park.

BOB. Not our little princess.

LIZ. Not our sweet Lillie; she's Grandma's girl.

STACIE. Hi, Mom! Hi, Dad! How can I help you get ready for the party?

LIZ. Hi, baby! Where's Lillie and Rod?

BOB. And Jack?

STACIE. They dropped me off and ran to get some ice cream. I asked Rod to do that because I didn't want Lillie here too early. The party won't be as exciting for her if she has to decorate for it herself.

LIZ. Okay.

Liz shakes her head, like she thinks her daughter might just be nuts.

BOB. Did Lillie invite any friends?

STACIE. No, she wanted to have her birthday party with just family.

BOB. And why wouldn't she? She has the most awesome family ever.

LIZ. Yes, she does! Okay, we're ready to party.

Steve, Michelle, Mike, and Toby come walking in.

STEVE. That's good, 'cause we're here.

The excited grandparents and kids hug and greet each other.

STEVE. Where's the birthday girl?

STACIE. She'll be here any minute.

BOB. Yep, and we're still waiting on Beth too.

Beth comes walking in.

BETH. I'm here, I'm here; how late am I?

STACIE. You're not late, sis; we're just counting heads.

LIZ. Okay, Lillie will be here any minute. Even though she knows it's her birthday party, let's make it a surprise. Everyone start singing when they walk in.

STACIE, *looking out the window.* Okay, here they come.

Lillie, Rod, and Jack walk in, and the family sings "Happy Birthday."

The family cheers, and they gather around the table, hold hands, and bow their heads to pray before they eat.

Black out.

NARRATOR. Well, that seems like a pretty normal family thing to do. They prayed before they ate and acknowledged God for their blessings. They clearly love each other; there wasn't one family fight or disagreement. Let's keep watching.

Scene 2

Liz, Bob, and Beth are cleaning up and chatting.

Liz. Oh, that was so much fun! I haven't had a little girl birthday party since you girls were small.

Beth. I remember our birthday parties; we were always competing to see who could have the most friends.

Liz. And the biggest cake.

Beth. Michelle won that; do you remember her Ferris wheel cake?

Bob. Remember it? I made it.

Liz. Your dad worked on the design for that cake for weeks.

Bob. I had trouble figuring out how to get the wheel to spin without tipping over the seats.

Liz. The frosting was nuts; I had to do that.

Beth. It wasn't fair that she won, you know.

Liz. You're just jealous because you didn't think to ask for something like that.

Beth. Whatever, Mom.

The phone rings.

Liz. Hello? Yes? (*Sounding a little more and more concerned with each word.*) Yes. What? Where? Well, how? Okay, thank you.

She hangs up.

LIZ. Bob! Bob! It's Lillie! Rod and Stacie were in a car accident on the way home; everyone is okay, except Lillie. They are rushing her to the hospital; we have to go now!

BOB. I'll go get the car.

BETH. Go, Dad. I'll help Mom get her things.

Beth gathers up her mother's things, helps her get her coat on, and keeps her focused on getting out with everything she needs, while Bob runs out to get the car. Beth helps her mother exit the stage; they are in panic and shock.

Black out.

Scene 3

In the waiting room of a hospital, Bob prays with the family. Everyone is present, except for Lillie.

BOB. Our dear heavenly Father, who loves us more than we could ever know, we come before You now in our deepest hour of need. Our hearts are so heavy with the pain of our dear Lillie, lying in surgery. We know things are very serious for her, and we are sad. We also know, God, that You are with her. Your Word tells us that You are ever present and all-knowing. No one understands this situation like You do. Only You understand its purpose, and only You can bring good things from this tragedy, joy from this pain. We ask for Your mercy and for Your healing for Lillie. Please, God, if it be Your will, don't take this child from us.

The room goes silent as some silently pray, some hold each other; all are visibly shaken and sad.

The doctor enters the room and stands at the corner of the circle where the family prays. He pauses, removing his surgery hat. When Rod sees the doctor, he stands, anticipating the news he brings.

DOCTOR. Mr. Jones, Lillie was injured very badly; we did everything we could to stop the bleeding and keep her alive, but we couldn't. Lillie didn't survive the surgery. I'm so sorry.

Rod shakes the doctor's hand, but he cannot contain his emotion; he cries, and the doctor comforts him with a hug. Rod then turns to Stacie and holds her close, bringing in Jake. Michelle and Beth hold the other children, and the family cries together.

Black out.

NARRATOR. I guess it's pretty clear that bad things do happen to good people, to Christian people. It seems that neither God nor the devil discriminates. Every family on earth experiences pain. I wonder if this terrible tragedy is enough to steal the joy from this Christian family. I've heard it said that God will guide Christians through life if they just trust and believe. Can a family still trust and believe when it seems that life couldn't be more unfair?

Scene 4

Beth is at Bob and Liz's house, having tea and chatting with her parents.

LIZ. How is Jason doing, dear? Have you heard from him since he left last week?

BETH. Yes, we Skyped last night. He's going to be deployed for six months this time, but he's supposed to be home for a couple of years after that.

BOB. That's great! It was great to see him this time; that six months he was here went by so fast.

LIZ. Yes, it did. You know, it's hard to believe that Lillie's been gone for six months.

BETH. I know. I was so glad they let Jason come home for the funeral. I didn't realize how much I would need him there.

BOB. Our God is so good to give us the people we need in our lives right when we need them most. God always provides for us. He always has; I know He always will.

BETH. He has always provided for me. I guess He's really all I need, but I am glad I have family.

"Jesus Is All I Need" is performed by Bob, Liz, and Beth.

LIZ. Do you want to stay for dinner, dear?

BETH. No, Momma, I'm going to go back to the apartment and go for a run. I have to work tomorrow, so I need to get to bed early tonight.

BOB. Are you still enjoying your job?

BETH. Yes, I like it. I get a little bored answering the phone all day, but I enjoy getting to visit with people.

LIZ. Are you thinking about getting a job in your field, now that you've finished college?

BETH. Oh, I suppose I could, but I'm content doing what I'm doing. My hours are nice, and I'm off in time to enjoy my evening. I never know when Jason is available to Skype with me, and this job lets me be flexible so I don't miss his calls. I'm just enjoying life, Mom; don't guilt me into working harder.

Beth kisses her mom and dad on the cheek to say goodbye and exits.

BOB. That girl has no initiative; she just rides through life by the seat of her pants.

LIZ. Bob, she just has an easy-going personality. She has no fears, no worries, no anxiety. It would be nice to be able to live that kind of life.

BOB. I suppose.

Lights out, and a spotlight comes up on a solo mic, where Beth sings "Nothing's Worrying Me."

Black out.

Scene 5

At Michelle and Steve's house, all the kids are there. Jack is staying all night with his cousins, Toby and Mike. Toby and Jack are playing a video game. Mike is pouting because he wants to play, but not that game.

MICHELLE. How's it going, boys? Are you having fun?

TOBY. Mike's not; he's pouting.

MIKE. I am not.

TOBY. Yes, he is, Mom! He's pouting because he doesn't want to play this game, but Jack and I want to play this game because we don't get to play it very often.

MIKE. That's not fair. I wanted to play Mario.

MICHELLE. Boys, please stop fighting. Look, it's not very often that you cousins all get to stay together overnight. We should enjoy each other's company, not fight.

Toby starts to cry.

MICHELLE. Toby, what's wrong?

TOBY. We're not all here. Lillie's not here.

Michelle holds Toby, and she and Steve look at each other as if trying to decide what to say.

STEVE. I know it doesn't make any sense. We don't understand why Lillie had to leave us, but we do know this: God is in control. If we simply trust Him, just trust Him, He will take care of us. We will always miss Lillie and be sad that we didn't get to watch her grow up, but one day, we will see how God can use something as sad and painful to us as Lillie's death to bring some joy and understanding to the lives of others.

MIKE. But why didn't He protect Lillie?

MICHELLE. Oh, honey, I don't know why He allowed her to die, but I do know that He did protect her. God was with her every minute of the accident, and all during the surgery, holding her, keeping her from pain, taking away her fears, letting her know that even though she wasn't going to be on this earth anymore, she was safe in His arms. You and I feel the pain of losing her because we miss her. But God even takes care of that. He promises us that we will see her again, in heaven.

STEVE. What do you think we could do to help us remember Lillie and help us heal the pain we feel from missing her?

TOBY. I look at pictures of her, but that makes me feel sad.

MIKE. We miss her, but probably not as much as Jack does.

MICHELLE. Jack, what do you do to help you not feel sad all the time about Lillie?

JACK. I pray.

MIKE. What good does that do? God let her die.

MICHELLE. Oh honey, this is very hard, isn't it? We all know that God didn't cause Lillie's death, but He did allow it to happen. There are lots of things both good and bad that come from Lillie's death. The bad is that we will miss her forever; we will always wonder what she would have looked like as a grown-up, who she would have married, what she would be in life.

STEVE. The good news is that we will get all of those answers one day, when we see her again. Lillie was a child, and we know from God's Word that she will be in heaven with Jesus. We don't know why our family had this happen, but we have each other to help us all get through it. God often uses difficult things in our lives for good. Someday, this experience will help us get through something else, or it will help us be able to help someone else. Jack has it right when he says he prays. Only God can enlighten you to understanding, and only He can bring you peace.

"I Pray" is sung by Jack or Michelle or Steve.

At the end of the song, all kids kneel together with Michelle and Steve, and they pray.

NARRATOR. Only God can enlighten us to understanding; only God can bring peace. Those are big words, big promises. I looked it up to be sure what I'm hearing our Christian family here say is correct:

Children go to heaven: "He called a little child and had him stand among them. And He said, I tell you the truth, unless you change and become the little children, you will never enter the kingdom of heaven. Therefore, whoever humbles himself like this child is the greatest in the kingdom of heaven" (Matthew 18:2–6).

God brings understanding: "But it is the spirit in a man, the breath of the Almighty that gives him understanding" (Job 32:8).

God brings peace: "The Lord gives strength to His people, the Lord blesses His people with peace" (Psalm 29:11).

So Christians pray, even in the face of adversity, for peace and understanding, and God's promises. What else can God do?

Scene 6

Stacie, Rod, and Jack at Liz and Bob's house.

STACIE. Hey, Momma!

JACK. Hi, Grammy and Pop!

He sits on Bob's lap.

BOB. How's my boy?

LIZ. Hi, baby! Hi, Rod. What are you doing here? We didn't know you were coming by.

STACIE. Well, we have some news.

ROD. Big news: we've bought a bigger house.

STACIE. And it's just down the street.

LIZ. What? Why?

BOB. I thought you liked your house.

ROD and STACIE. We do.

STACIE. But, well, we've been talking about trying to have another child.

ROD. We know that no one could ever replace Lillie, but we feel that we have enough love, and room, to have a bigger family.

BOB. So why a bigger house?

ROD. Well, you know what God told Noah.

LIZ, *looking very confused.* What?

Bob. I think you've got your Bible stories confused. God told Noah to build an ark, not have a baby or buy a house.

Rod. That's true, and I'm talking about the ark.

Liz. The ark?

Rod. Yes. Noah gave an example for us all; when God says build an ark, it won't be just another rainy day.

Liz, *still very confused*. Is it going to rain?

Stacie. No, Momma; what Rod is *trying* to tell you is that we are going to have a baby, and we will need a bigger house.

Liz and Bob. Yay, we're so happy for you.

After some hugs and rejoicing, Liz realizes that she's still confused.

Liz. I don't get it; why do you have to have bigger house? Can't you use the bedroom that was Lillie's?

Stacie. No, Momma, we wouldn't mind using Lillie's room, but it's not big enough for triplets!

"Just Another Rainy Day" is sung by the cast; we had Michelle and Steve come in and sing it and the kids danced (the three boys, representing the triplets) with matching animal heads (representing the animals in the ark). They had three sets of matching heads: lions, zebras, and giraffes. Very cute!

Narrator. Wow! God did bless them mightily, didn't He? What more could this family have to look forward to? Much like Job, this family has suffered great loss, but because they were faithful to God throughout the trial and trusted Him to get them through it, God was faithful to bless them more than before! Not that any one child could ever be replaced, but all children are blessings, and three at one time—well, that is significant, isn't it? So we've established that Christianity happens by believing in the Lord Jesus Christ.

We've also discovered that trusting God to lead you through the trials of life is the only way to get through those trials successfully. The Bible also tells us that there is more to come. The story doesn't end with Jesus's birth, death, and resurrection; He promises that He will return to earth to take His children home. 1 Thessalonians 4:16–18 says, "For the Lord himself will come down from heaven with a loud command, with the voice of the archangel, and with the trumpet call of God, and the dead in Christ will rise first. After that, we who are still alive and are left will be caught up together with them in the clouds to meet the Lord in the air. And so we will be with the Lord forever. Therefore, encourage each other with these words." So Jesus will return to gather up His children to be with Him forever in heaven. Who are His children? The Christians.

Scene 7

Leaving church Easter Sunday morning.

STEVE. That was a wonderful Easter morning church service.

MICHELLE. Yes, it was.

BOB. You know, I love Easter, but I've got to tell you: I am looking forward to that great reunion day.

LIZ. The great resurrection morning.

TOBY. When we see Jesus?

ROD. Yes, when we see Jesus.

JACK. And we see Lillie.

"The Resurrection Morn" is sung by the cast.

A Christmas Story to Remember

This is a really fun play about parents who use the characters their kids are already familiar with to recite the Christmas story in a way their kids will never forget. While the script isn't terribly long, it takes about an hour by the time everything is acted out accordingly.

Cast

Mom: an adult

Dad: an adult

A catlike superhero: any age (Find someone who can do a front walkover.)

A beautiful female warrior: any age (We used an adult.)

A male warrior: any age (We used an adult.)

An adventurer: any age (This person needs to be of similar age to the beautiful female warrior.)

An angel: any age (Use the same actor as used for the catlike superhero here.)

Impossible mission messenger: any age

Donkey: any age (A rubber donkey mask can be used.)

Farmer man: any age

Farmer woman: any age (She needs to be of similar age to the farmer man.)

An alien: any age (A rubber Martian mask can be used.)

Stooge one: any age

Stooge two: any age

Stooge three: any age

A caped/mustached villain: any age

Kids: (The kids who were the stooges, the Martian, the donkey, and those who didn't have parts were used; you use who you have.)

A Christmas Story to Remember cast

The stage is a living room scene with Christmas tree lights on. A mom enters (obviously in the middle of the night) doing her best Santa work. She fluffs bows and places packages, fills stockings, and so on. From the opposite side of the room, Dad enters, wheeling in a bicycle. Because he's backing into the room, he doesn't realize she has her back to him, and they back into each other, scream with a start, and quickly shush each other so as not to wake the children. They have a few more bumbles, such as a bicycle that won't stand up on its kickstand. As they look around the room to see how things look, they realize they have forgotten to eat the cookies and quickly begin to argue over who has to eat them; after a quick game of rock-paper-scissors, the loser (Mom) has to eat the cookies, and the second loser (Dad) has to drink the milk. Dad doesn't like milk, and he is obviously anxious about having to drink it. He shifts his weight and rubs his head and finally gulps it down with a horrible look on his face. Mom throws her cookies in the trash and just looks at him as if to say, "Really? You couldn't find the sink?"

Mom sits down and looks at the work they've done to make Christmas special; after a bit, she starts to cry. Dad gets visibly nervous, thinking he's done something terribly wrong. Finally, he makes an attempt to comfort her.

DAD. What's wrong?

MOM. I'm just so discouraged. I mean, I love Christmas and all of the festivities that go along with it, but I feel as though we just aren't making the purpose of it clear to the kids. How do we get through to them that what we are celebrating is Jesus?

DAD. We read the Christmas story every year.

MOM. I know we do, but they don't listen, I mean *really* listen. I'm just not sure they get it. Isn't there something we can do to make it more exciting for them? I mean, those kids can describe the detail of every video game, they know every cartoon and Disney character, and they quote the motto of every superhero ever made. But ask them what gifts the wise men brought, and they look at you like you're crazy.

DAD, *after some thought*. So why don't we tell the story with characters they know?

MOM, *after a beat*. What?

DAD. You know, Mary and Joseph are superheroes on a mission.

MOM, *looking at him like he might just be nuts.* What?

DAD. They would love it, and I bet you anything they'd remember the story. When they remember the story, they'll begin to really understand what it is we're celebrating and why it's so magical and wonderful.

MOM. Hmmm, you might just be right. Okay, how do we this?

DAD. Well, I would start with Mary, don't you think?

The lighting shifts a little as the spotlight will begin to focus on the characters who act out the story Mom and Dad are telling.

MOM. Okay, so we make Mary a secret superhero? What kind of superhero is she?

DAD. Like a cat woman superhero who wears all black and has a long tail.

He raises his eyebrows, as if he's thinking of a most attractive black leather cat outfit.

A female cat superhero walks out and awaits her direction.

MOM. No, Mary isn't a cat. (*The cat character backs off the stage.*) She's more like a woman from an Amazon tribe! A female warrior who is beautiful, smart, and good-hearted, and she always fights evil.

The female warrior comes out, looking confident and strong.

DAD. I can see that.

MOM AND DAD. The beautiful warrior woman it is.

MOM. Okay, so we tell the story. Mary is a beautiful young woman who loved God very much. God looked down on her and was so pleased with her that He sent—what do you think? A mighty warrior? (*Dad nods.*) Yes, a mighty warrior, like Hercules, to see her and grant her a very special gift.

A mighty warrior comes out.

WARRIOR. Mary, you have been chosen by God to fulfill a special mission. You have been faithful to Him all of your life, and He has selected you to be the mother of His only Son.

MOM. Although Mary was a little confused, and she was worried that her fiancé would not understand, she was also very grateful to have been asked by God to do such a wonderful thing. She thanked the warrior for bringing her the news.

Mary thanks the warrior, and he exits.

DAD. So Mary goes over to see Joseph and tell him about the news she received.

Joseph enters and Mary approaches him. He is dressed in tan pants, a brown leather bomber jacket, a tan or brown leather hat, and a rope looped on his waistband, as though he is ready for an archeological adventure.

MARY. Joseph! (*They greet each other with a warm hug and appear very happy to see each other.*) I have some very exciting news.

MOM. Joseph tries to be kind, but he is clearly confused and disappointed to hear that Mary will be having a baby. After all, they aren't even married yet; what will people think?

Joseph puts his head down and slowly steps away; he reaches out affectionately toward Mary before walking off one side of the stage. Mary then leaves in the opposite direction.

MOM. God knew this would be hard for Joseph to understand.

Joseph walks out toward the center, pacing.

MOM. So He sent an angel to see Joseph and explain what's going on and what Joseph needs to do.

Angel walks out; it's obviously the same actor who was the cat superhero.

DAD. No, not an angel.

The angel looks back at Dad like, "Really?" *She throws her arms up and stomps off the stage.*

DAD. He sends a dude with briefcase and a black suit who brings him a message about a mission he must complete, if he chooses.

Music plays as Joseph, facing the audience, opens the briefcase so only he can see it. On the screen at the back of the stage, we see a man appear on video.

MAN. Joseph, you have been selected for a very special mission. God has chosen your betrothed to be the mother of His only Son. That will make you, Joseph, the earthly father of the Lord and Savior, Jesus. Your mission, should you choose to accept it, will be to protect this child and ensure He is able to escape the wrath of Satan, who will use many kings and governmental leaders to try to kill Him. While Jesus is a child, you will need to protect Him. God will be with you every step of the way, guiding you. This message will self-destruct in five seconds.

Joseph slams the briefcase shut and throws it off-stage, looking scared and horrified. He runs the other way, and the screen shows a bomb blowing up.

DAD. Joseph is like a history professor ready for a real-life mission. He felt really proud that God wanted him to be part of this wonderful plan. (*Joseph stands up straight and tall.*) He could hardly wait to get to Mary and tell her how excited he was about what they were about to experience.

MOM. Great! This is really shaping up; I think the kids will love it. Okay, what happens next? Oh, they have to go to Bethlehem to register for the census. So they travel by donkey because Mary is almost ready to have the baby, and the trip is hard for her. (*A very pregnant Mary and Joseph, holding hands, walk out on stage with donkey.*) Finally, they get to Bethlehem and knock on the door of the local Holiday Inn, but there isn't any room there, so the hotel clerk tells them they can stay in the barn. Mary walks into the barn and uses her superpowers to set up a lovely sleeping area for herself, Joseph, and the soon-to-be-born Son of God.

Mary does a spin and pose, and the lights go down.

Two farmers, a man and a woman, walk out on stage. The man has a pitchfork and wears overalls; the woman wears her hair in a bun and has on an old farm dress. Neither smile.

DAD. Out in the fields of a nearby land, some farmers were working outside, taking care of their sheep and cows, when one of them suddenly saw a UFO. (*The farmers look up to the sky with no change in their expression. Suddenly, a Martian appears.*) The Martian tells the farmers of the Lord Jesus, who will be born in a manger in a stable in Bethlehem, and explains where to go and find Him.

The alien mimes speaking while Dad tell the story and then leaves the stage. The farmers begin their journey, leaving the stage in the opposite direction.

MOM. Yes, that's good. Now, back at the barn, Mary has had the baby and is loving on Him, like all new mothers do. (*Mary is sitting on the front of the stage, rocking the baby.*) Joseph is on high alert, knowing that the Mary has fulfilled the big part of her mission, but his part, keeping Mary and the baby safe, is still ahead of him.

Joseph looks around and appears to be on guard. He assists Mary to her feet and follows her off stage, peering back out at the audience before completely leaving.

DAD. In another faraway land, three stooges lived in a palace.

MOM. What? What are you talking about?

DAD. Just stick with me here. Three men, who happened to be very silly brothers, lived in a palace. Despite their silly demeanor, they were actually quite intelligent and liked to watch the sky and learn about the stars.

The first one comes out looking through a handheld telescope to the sky; the other two are right behind him and bump into him.

MOM. Oh, okay. I see where this is going; the three wise men, right?

DAD. Yes! So as the first stooge was watching the stars one night, he noticed one that seemed particularly bright, so bright in fact that he felt completely compelled to follow it. He knew in his heart of hearts that it was some kind of wonderful sign and that the star would lead them to the long-awaited King.

STOOGE 2. What 'cha doing?

STOOGE 1. I'm looking at the stars; one is really huge. I think we should follow it.

Stooges 2 and 3 look at each other and shrug like, "Okay, whatever." Stooge 1 starts walking, looking through his handheld telescope, and Stooges 2 and 3 follow, also looking up. Stooge 1 stops, and Stooge 3 runs into Stooge 1, and Stooge 2 runs into Stooge 3.

STOOGE 1. Why, I oughtta …

He thumps Stooge 3 on the head, who in turn thumps Stooge 2 on the head (who is sad because he has no one to thump).

STOOGE 1. Come on.

Stooges 2 and 3 look up to the sky again but begin following the wrong stars. Stooge 1 looks back and sees them walking away.

STOOGE 1. Hey, where are you going?

Stooge 2 and 3 look at each other and shrug; they walk back to get in line behind Stooge 1.

STOOGE 1. Who's leading this expedition, me or you?

STOOGE 3. I think I should.

STOOGE 2. I think we should play rock-paper-scissors to see who leads.

They all nod, and they begin. Stooge 1 leads the way as they say, "Rock, paper, scissors." They all draw rock. "Rock, paper, scissors." They all draw paper. "Rock, paper, scissors." They all draw scissors.

STOOGE 1, *slapping Stooge 2*. You numbskull!

STOOGE 2, *poking Stooge 1 in the eyes*. Cut it out.

STOOGE 1. Ah wise guy, eh?

He winds up and punches Stooge 2, who ducks behind Stooge 3, and Stooge 3 gets punched. Stooge 3 makes an angry huff at the audience and winds up to punch Stooge 2, who is now behind him, but Stooge 1 interrupts.

STOOGE 1. Come on, guys. Let's go; we have a star to follow.

The stooges all leave the stage.

Dad laughs out loud; he loves this kind of comedy.

MOM. That's really cute. I like it, hon. Good job! Okay, we need to get back to the story of Jesus and what's happening with Him. Joseph, remember, is thinking about his mission and how he is going to keep this baby and His mother safe.

DAD. Yes, Joseph is a very social guy. Being a carpenter in the community, he knows everyone and hears all the latest news. He knows that King Herod is calling for the death of babies because he fears the Messiah will be born soon.

MOM. Yes, Herod is an evil character who is friends with the devil and plots evil against anyone he feels opposes his plans to control the country.

An evil King Herod comes out and prances across the stage, stopping in the center to wink at the audience while he strokes his long handlebar mustache. He is dressed in a black suit with tuxedo tails and a black top hat.

DAD, *while the character is standing center stage.* Who is that?

MOM. That's our evil villain; he's King Herod.

DAD. Are these kids gonna know who that is?

MOM. Sure, he's the guy who ties young maidens to railroad tracks. Remember the evil magician in the *Frosty the Snowman* movie, the one who was trying to steal Frosty's magical hat?

DAD. Yeah, I remember him.

MOM. Well, he's kind of like that.

DAD. Okay, that's good.

MOM. It is good, isn't it?

King Herod exits.

DAD. It is. I think the kids are going to love this story.

Mom. I think the kids are going to remember this story. And you know what else? Even if we don't get the total truth through to them today, the story is so interesting and fun, we can continue to talk about it throughout the year.

Dad. That's true. I bet Holland talks about Mary the warrior all year long.

Mom. She will. And when she does, we can point out how God made all that happen so Jesus could be born and one day, thirty-three years later, become the Savior of the world.

Dad. Our Savior.

Mom. Yes, our Savior.

Mom and Dad have a lovely moment of just cuddling on the sofa, proud of the story they've developed to share with their children.

Dad, *looking at his watch*. Don't you think we had better try to get some sleep before the kids get up?

Mom. Yes, we should; let's go.

Just then, the kids all come running in, cheering and yelling.

Mom and Dad yell, "Merry Christmas," and then work to calm them down.

Dad. Okay, kids, you can all open one present.

The kids quickly open one present (all at the same time); they love their gifts, say thank you, and give their parents hugs.

Mom. Okay, everyone, gather around. It's time to talk about what Christmas is all about.

The kids gather around and get quiet. Mom and Dad look at each and then at the kids.

MOM AND DAD. Have we got a story for you.

KHLY Radio Christmas

This story makes several references to our local community in many of the radio briefings. Feel free to edit to accommodate your own hometown feel. You can use musical tracks, but if you have your own musicians, you have more freedom. Feel free to borrow from other small churches in the area; most musicians love the opportunity to get to participate.

Cast

Big Mike: a loudmouthed, bossy man who runs a radio station and sometimes takes his authoritarian attitude home to the family

Roberta: Mike's loving and devoted wife

DJ Jon: a Christian man who works as a DJ for a local radio station

Becky: Jon's loving and supportive wife

Dayton and Beau: Mike and Roberta's sons

Shelby and Holland: Mike and Roberta's daughters

Jake Neutron: traffic and weather reporter

Tom and Huck: radio show duo

Alex Bailey: news reporter

Glenn: a poker buddy

Robby: a poker buddy (young and inexperienced)

Frank: a poker buddy God uses to show a change of heart and attitude

Dad: Mike's deceased father

Angel: a big, tough angel who looks like a motorcycle dude

Homer Branscum as DJ Jon in KHLY Radio

Scene 1

A sparkly soloist comes on stage and sings a peppy version of "*O Little Town*" (we used Amy Grant's version of the song).

Lights down, and lights up on the radio station booth, where a DJ begins to speak.

DJ Jon. Merry Christmas and good afternoon, Heber Springs; this is DJ Jon with KHLY Radio, bringing you the best Christmas music in the entire state of Arkansas. Tonight, remember that there is a Christmas play at the high school at 7:00 p.m. Also tonight, the Forty-Second Baptist

Church will have Christmas caroling that begins at the local nursing home and ends up at the Courthouse Square. So as you are out driving around tonight looking at Christmas lights, slow down your driving, roll down your windows, and listen to the carolers sing. That's right, ladies and gentlemen, I said slow and roll. Now for a little bluegrass Christmas from our local band, the Kolt 45s.

Lights down on the radio booth and up on the musicians, who play a bluegrass version of "Jingle Bells."

Scene 2

Lights down on the musicians and up on Big Mike, who sits behind his desk, listening to the radio station he owns.

Big Mike. That's better! What is the matter with that DJ? Who does he think he is, playing Christian Christmas music? I'm the owner of this radio station, and I say that while Christmas music is fine, Christian Christmas music is not. We'll lose our entire audience. I'm gonna call up there right now and tell him to knock it off before I knock him off.

Mike dials the phone; we hear it ring, and a spotlight comes up on DJ Jon, who picks up the phone. It's not Mike's call he gets; he stays on the phone, talking to a listener.

Jon. KHLY Radio, this is DJ Jon, playing all your Christmas special requests. Is there something I can play for you?

Diane. I want to hear Jennifer's version of "One King."

DJ Jon. Great, I can do that. Tell me why that song is so special to you.

Diane. Well, last year at Christmastime, I was really struggling in life. I was out of a job, my marriage was on the rocks, and I just felt as though nothing would ever be okay again. But then I heard this song. There was something about this version that made me hear the words and understand the meaning. Suddenly, I understood that Christmas isn't about what I can or cannot afford to buy my family, or how I might celebrate with friends. Christmas is a celebration all its own. Christmas is a gift to us. I don't know; I didn't explain that well, but this song changed me, and I want to listen to it every year at Christmas for as long as I live.

JON. Wow, that is a great story, caller; do you mind if I ask your name?

DIANE. This is Diane.

Jon. Well, Diane, here is your song.

Lights down on the stage and up on the musicians, as Jennifer sings *"One King."*

Lights down on the musicians and up on Big Mike and DJ Jon; we hear the phone ring again.

JON. KHLY Radio, this is DJ Jon playing all your Christmas special requests; is there something I can play for you?

MIKE. Is there something you can play for me? Is there something you can play for me? I know something you can stop playing for me! This is Mike Berretski, the owner of KHLY, and your boss. I'm asking you to play what you are supposed to be playing. I demand that you stop playing that Christian Christmas music. This is not a Christian radio station; this is a popular music radio station. We have the biggest audience in the entire state of Arkansas, and you are going to blow it with your self-centered gospel music antics! Are you listening to me?

JON. Yes, sir.

MIKE. If I hear any more of that garbage, I'll come down there in person; do you understand me?

JON. Yes, sir. Um … sir?

MIKE. What is it?

JON. Can I play songs people call in and request?

MIKE. Yes, you can, during request hours.

Mike hangs up the phone.

JON. Thank you.

He looks at his phone, realizing he's been hung up on, and places it back on the receiver; lights down on Jon.

MIKE. I can't believe that idiot; who does he think he is, changing the playlist like that? (*He stands up, stretches, and then rubs his belly.*) Whoo, I'm hungry. Hey Roberta, what's for dinner?

Scene 3

Lights out on Mike and up on the DJ booth for a quick weather and traffic report.

JAKE. This is Jake Neutron with your traffic and weather report. It looks like another cold one, with lows in the 40s. Tomorrow is a high of 53 and a low of 45. Traffic tonight is all clear except for a wreck on 67 South toward Little Rock. That's it for your weather and traffic; now back to your music.

Lights out on the DJ booth and up on the musicians, who play a Christmas tune while a scene change takes place.

Lights out on the musicians and up on the stage, where we see Mike and his family gathered at the dinner table.

MIKE, *opening the casserole lid*. What's for dinner?

ROBERTA. I made chicken casserole and salad, and the kids made a dessert.

MIKE. Good, I'm starved.

DAYTON. We made dessert, Dad. You're really gonna be surprised.

MIKE, *completely uninterested.* Yeah.

BEAU. We won our basketball game today, Dad. I scored ten points.

MIKE. Uh huh.

SHELBY. Hey, Dad, can we advertise for our Girl Scout troop on your radio station? We have to find a way to sell more cookies.

HOLLAND. Yeah, can we?

MIKE. Uh huh, that's good.

ROBERTA. Speaking of the radio station, the music was really good today. I love the new Christmas format. (*Her speaking slows a bit, as she sees the temper in Mike rise.*)

MIKE. What do you mean, the music was really good today? Did you hear what was being played? He had gospel songs on all day. Why would he do that? Why would you like that? You're so stupid. Did you call up there and ask him to play that garbage? Do you know anything? Gospel music is not what we want to hear. It is not what the people want to hear. Don't tell anyone that you enjoy that music. And if you do, don't tell them you know me; my wife needs to have better taste than that.

Mike storms off, knocking over his chair. The family is, of course, devastated. Mom quickly springs into action, holding back her tears as she comforts her children and encourages them to continue their dinner, assuring them all is well.

ROBERTA. It's okay, kids; it's okay. He's had a stressful day at work; things are hectic at the radio station. It's okay. Let's just enjoy the rest of our dinner, and then we'll have some yummy dessert in a bit, okay?

SHELBY. Dad didn't stay to eat any of Dayton's dessert.

DAYTON. It's okay, Shelby. I'll take him some later when he's not mad about work anymore.

ROBERTA. Good idea.

The family continues to eat dinner; the lights go out on them and up on the musicians, who play another Christmas song for a scene change.

Scene 4

Lights out on musicians and up on the living room of DJ Jon and his wife. Jon comes walking in from work as Becky is wrapping some gifts.

JON. Hi, honey.

BECKY. Well, hello, honey. How was your day? I love the Christmas songs that you played today; the request segment was so good. I just wrapped presents all day and sang along. Christmas is my favorite time of the year.

JON. I love those songs too, Becky, but I'm going to get fired if I keep playing them.

BECKY. What do you mean, fired?

JON. Big Mike called the station today, and he was really upset. He said that our radio station has no business playing Christian Christmas music. He said he wants to hear songs about snowmen, reindeer, and elves; he doesn't want to hear about babies and wise men. He said if I wanted to keep playing that music, I had to go somewhere else to work. He said this is a pop music station, and he is not going to have Christian Christmas music on his radio station.

BECKY. I don't get it; doesn't he understand what Christmas is about? It's not about snowmen and reindeer and elves; it's not even about shopping. It is Jesus's birthday."

JON. I don't think he knows, nor do I think he cares. He said if he tunes in again and hears Christian Christmas music, well, Becky, I'm going to lose my job.

BECKY. What are you going to do?

JON. I don't know. Most of the audience is requesting Christian Christmas music. That's most of my show. That's what they request; that's what I play; that's what they want to hear.

BECKY. Did you tell him that? Maybe he just doesn't realize.

JON. I did. I asked very specifically if I can play the music that is requested.

BECKY. Good! What did he say?

JON. He said yes.

BECKY. Well, then, there you go; play it.

JON. I don't know, Becky; his prior message was *very* clear.

BECKY. Listen, Jon, people give mixed messages all the time, but God doesn't send us mixed messages. His Word is very clear, and He will guide us through this confusing time. You know what to do here; you know right from wrong. We just need to pray that Mike begins to understand it too.

JON. You are absolutely right.

BECKY. Let's just stop right now and pray; let's pray that God intervenes in Mike's life.

They stand and hold hands, and Becky leads the prayer.

BECKY. Dear Lord, we praise Your name, and we thank You for the magnitude of Your love and mercy in our lives. You have never failed to provide for us. Today, we find ourselves in a situation with Mike Betowski.

JON. Berretski.

BECKY. Whatever; God knows who I'm talking about. He threatened to fire Jon today for playing music that glorifies You and tells the story of You, Lord, the real story of Jesus. We ask that You intervene in Mike's life and change his heart, Lord. Whether he fires Jon or not, Mike needs You in his life. Lord, I pray that You use us in a mighty way.

JON. Thank You, God. I ask that You help me to be fearless and strong. Amen.

Lights out on Jon and Becky and up on the musicians for the song "Why I Love Christmas."

Scene 5

Lights out on the musicians and up on the stage, where we see a poker game in process.

Robby is dealing out the cards.

MIKE. Five, Robby; one, two, three, four … five.

GLENN. This time I better get a good hand.

ROBBY. Was that five?

GLENN and FRANK. That was four.

MIKE. There you go, Robby.

ROBBY. All right, Big Mike; you're up.

MIKE. Hmm. Well, you can do one thing, Robby: You gave me some good cards! I bet seven.

FRANK. I'll see that.

He throws his chips on the table.

MIKE. Now Glenn's gonna fold.

GLENN. I fold.

MIKE. That's what I thought.

ROBBY. Okay now, let me see.

Beau and Dayton come walking in, and Mike gets all excited.

MIKE. Boys! Hey, guys, my boys are here. Come on over here and see your ol' dad. Now, let me teach you a thing or two about poker. I'll have you swindling your friends before you're teenagers. You'll be rich!

DAYTON. Dad, we just came down to say good night.

MIKE. Good night? It's only midnight; we've got a few more hands to play. Hey, Dayton, why don't you run out to the garage and get me and the fellas more beer while I teach Beau here how to play a winning hand.

FRANK. Come on, Mike; it's pretty late. You should let those boys go to bed.

MIKE. What are you saying, Frank? You don't think I know how to raise my boys?

Mike and Frank both stand and seem ready to fight each other, but Glenn is in the chair between them. In the meantime, Robby starts flailing about, trying to get out of the way of the possible fight—and capture some money from the table. He falls.

GLENN. Wait a minute, men; let's just hold on and calm down. Nobody is accusing anybody of anything. Robby, what are you doing?

Robby gets up, and everyone looks at him like he's nuts.

MIKE. You just get out of here, all of you! You're nothing but a bunch of jerks, anyway; get out and stay out. This is my house. Those are my kids. I'm the father. I'm Big Mike. Now, get out!

All of Mike's friends leave, and Mike is left alone in the room. He is still snorting around and throws some poker chips when he hears a voice.

DAD. Pick that up!

MIKE. Dad? I can't believe I'm seeing you. You've been dead for ten years.

DAD. I have? No wonder I feel so rested. What are you doing, Mike?

MIKE. What do you mean?

DAD. I mean, what are you doing? You've got a beautiful wife, you've got four wonderful children, and you're treating them like this?

MIKE. Well, I, uh, well, you see, um …

DAD. Listen, I know I wasn't the best father, but I did try. What you're doing, however, is ridiculous.

MIKE. What do you mean?

DAD. I mean, you come in here, acting like a big jerk, yelling at your family as if they caused your problems at work. You're picking fights with your friends, and then you have the idiotic idea to send your kids to the garage to get beer and teach them how to play poker. What do you have to say for yourself?

MIKE. Um, well, you see, uh, I …

DAD. If I catch you acting like this again, I'll come back to earth and knock you off it.

MIKE. Yes, sir.

Dad walks off.

MIKE, *standing still and then rubbing his eyes and his head.* I have got to go to bed. I'm going crazy.

Lights out on stage and up on musicians, who play a Christmas song for the scene change.

Scene 6

Lights out on musicians and up on the DJ booth, where we see two men.

HUCK, *on the phone.* Sure, we can leave that message for him; thank you."

He hangs up the phone.

DJ Jon walks in.

DJ JON. Hey guys; how's it going?

TOM. It's been a great show; the question is, are you ready for yours? The requests are coming in already.

HUCK. Yeah, we've had to tell some to call back.

JON. Well, I'm ready.

Tom and Huck leave, and DJ Jon approaches the booth, where he stops before he sits down.

Jon. Okay, God, You've got this.

He sits down, and the phone rings.

JON. KHLY Radio Christmas, this is DJ Jon; what can I play for you today?

He listens, nods his head, and writes down a song; lights out on Jon and up on the musicians, where a soloist sings "The Caroler's Song."

Scene 7

Lights out on the musicians and up on Big Mike in his office.

MIKE. I can't believe he's playing that music again; what is he thinking? I'm going to call down there right now and fire him. I'll take over the radio station myself if I have to.

Mike picks up the phone to dial (he stands because he's too mad to sit), and the lights come up on DJ Jon at the booth, on the phone. In the soft lighting, we see Becky at home on the sofa, reading her Bible and praying. Mike has to keep redialing.

JON. This is DJ Jon with another special request. This one comes from Lila. Lila wants to hear "Silent Night." There are so many requests coming in today that I may not have time to play them all; the phone hasn't stopped ringing, but I will do my best. Merry Christmas!

Lights up on the musicians as they play "Silent Night," and the spotlight hits Becky as she prays.

Lights out on Becky and musicians and up on Mike at his desk.

MIKE. I can't believe he's this busy. How can he be this busy? Listen to the music he's playing; these callers are probably trying to get him to play something decent.

Mike slams down his phone and growls with pure frustration.

Frank walks in.

FRANK. Hey, Mike, how are you doing?

MIKE. Hey, Frank.

They shake hands; after all, the last time they were together, there was almost a fight.

FRANK. Hey, I was just in town running some errands, and for some reason, I felt the need to come by and talk to you. I'm not really sure why; I just felt I had to. I want to tell you that I've really enjoyed the Christmas music you're playing this year. Yeah, uh, a few months ago, my wife and I started going to church, and the preacher talks a lot about Jesus and salvation and all the things that Christ did for us. I mean, think about it: He died for our sins. I have really struggled with the idea that He had to die for the sins that I've committed, not only in the past, but the ones I'll commit in my future.

Then, I think about Christmas being a celebration of His birth here on earth, and I get a little overwhelmed. Anyway, the music you've been playing is touching my heart, and you know me, Mike. I'm not a soft guy. I don't think I've ever shed a tear. It's just that I'm learning about God and how much He loves me. He loves all of us. It's been an incredible experience. I don't completely understand it, and I don't understand why I felt like I needed to come by and tell you about it. It's just that since you've been playing this music, I thought you'd understand. You're kind of a hard guy, like me, so I thought maybe you'd get it. Sometimes it's good to be able to just tell your friends about stuff like that, you know? Anyway, the music you're playing, it's changing me. I just wanted to say thank you.

Frank starts to walk away.

MIKE. Frank, tell me more about this birthday.

FRANK. Isn't it the most amazing thing you've ever heard? I mean, to think that God would send His only Son to earth to be born. (*Now he turns to face the audience and continues telling the story, while the children come out and set up the nativity.*) Picture it: God sent an angel to a young woman named Mary, who was engaged to a young man named Joseph. The angel told Mary that God had chosen her to be the mother of Emmanuel, God with us. He also told her that she was with child, that she would give birth to a Son, and that He would be called Jesus. Mary, of course, said, "How can this be? I've never even been with a man." And here's where the story gets interesting to me; how in the world is Joseph going to react? When he hears the news that his fiancée is pregnant, obviously Joseph is going to think that Mary has been unfaithful. But God took care of that too. He sent an angel to visit Joseph as well; he talked him through it, gave him advice, and gave him the strength to get through it. Joseph was a good guy and did the right thing, not because he was good, but because God is good.

Now that first Christmas Day was a truly magical event. It was filled with all sorts of obstacles for Mary and Joseph to overcome. To begin, they had to travel to Bethlehem for the census, and when they got there, they were exhausted. On top of that, there were no motel rooms available, so they wound up staying in a barn. Jesus was born there, and Mary and Joseph served as His earthly parents. It's incredible to unwind the entire Christmas story and identify all of the different miracles that took place and how God orchestrated it all. There was the story of Mary and Joseph, but there was also the story of the wise men, the story of the shepherds, the story of the angels, the census, and the innkeeper. There was so much going on, and it's all set against the backdrop of the evil King Herod, who wanted all of the babies killed because the prophets had foretold that the Savior would be born in Bethlehem.

Isn't it the most incredible story you've ever heard? I can look back on my own life and identify all sorts of times when God saved me from serious trouble, and I've got to tell you, it feels a lot better to know Him personally. Anyway, listen, I've got to run. Like I said, I don't really even know why I stopped by. I guess mostly to say thanks for the music, buddy.

MIKE. Thanks, Frank.

FRANK. You bet.

They shake hands, and Frank exits.

Lights out on the scene, with a single spot left only on Big Mike.

MIKE. Angels don't visit people; that's the stupidest thing I've ever heard. What an idiot.

The little angel from the manger scene walks over in front of Mike and shrugs her shoulders, as if to say, "Who knew?"

Lights out on Mike and up on the musicians for scene-change music.

Scene 8

Lights out on the musicians and up on the DJ booth.

ALEX. This is Alex Bailey, with your twenty-second news brief. Trump has made someone mad, Hillary is begging for a job in the Senate, phones are still exploding in people's pockets, and the latest round of explosions are tied to ISIS. Scientists have proven that black cats are indeed bad luck, and just fifteen minutes ago, Santa and his reindeer were spotted flying high over the Antarctic. This is Alex Bailey with your twenty-second news brief.

Lights out on Alex and up on the musicians for scene-change music.

Lights out on the musicians and up on Becky and Jon's living room.

Jon walks in with roses.

JON. Hey, Becky.

BECKY. Hi, Jon; how was your day?

JON. It was the most amazing day ever. I played so many requests today, and every single song was Christian Christmas music. The requests were coming in so fast that I had no chance to play anything else, and best of all, I didn't hear from Big Mike one time.

BECKY. I'm so glad. I've prayed for that man all day long.

They laugh together and hug; lights out.

Lights up on the musicians, where we hear a sleepy version of "Away in a Manger."

Scene 9

Lights out on the musicians and up on the stage, where we see Mike and Roberta asleep in their bed.

Angel walks in, and Mike awakens.

MIKE. What was that?

ANGEL. Have no fear, Mike Betowski.

MIKE. Berretski. (*Pulls his blankets up as if he's embarrassed to be seen in his PJs.*) Who are you? How'd you get in here?

ANGEL. I'm a messenger angel, and I've come to bring you news.

MIKE. Oh man, I'm having a dream.

ANGEL. No, no, Mike; you're not dreaming. The good news that was proclaimed in Bethlehem thousands of years ago is still good news for you today. Mike Berretski, today in the city of David, a Savior has been born. He will be for all people. Today is Christmas Day. Mike Berretski, Christ was born for you. He also died for you. This is your opportunity, Mike Berretski; will you accept Christ as your Savior? Will you believe?

The angel leaves. Mike rubs his eyes, looks around, and screams.

MIKE. Roberta!

Roberta jumps out of bed, looking frantic and scared.

Lights out on the bedroom and up on the musicians for a scene change.

Scene 10

Lights out on the musicians and up on the DJ booth, where we find Tom and Huck.

TOM. This is Tom.

HUCK. And this is Huck with your Christmas morning music.

TOM. We've heard Santa successfully made his trip through Heber Springs, and we're hoping to hear from you this morning.

HUCK. Yes, call us and tell us what Santa left in your stocking.

TOM. Call 866-4825, that's TOM-HUCK, or 866-4825.

Lights out on the DJ booth and up on the musicians for a round of "Happy Birthday."

Scene 11

Lights out on the musicians and up on center stage, where we see a sleepy Roberta and her children. They have stockings and are preparing to tear into them; she has coffee. Big Mike enters in a whole new kind of mood.

MIKE. It's Christmas morning, it's Christmas morning, it's Christmas morning! (*He kneels by the kids.*) Hey, kids, do you know what today is?

KIDS. It's Christmas morning.

MIKE. Do you know what today really is?

KIDS. Christmas morning.

MIKE. Do you know what today *really* is?

KIDS. Christmas morning.

MIKE. No, it's Jesus's birthday. (*He goes down the line, hugging each child.*) It's Jesus's birthday, it's Jesus's birthday, it's Jesus's birthday!

A very emotional scene takes place as Roberta realizes that something big has happened to Big Mike, and the family rejoices for a moment in this hope.

MIKE. So, guys, I was thinking, the guys at the radio station are working really hard today, and I think we should go down to the station and take them some breakfast to show them how much we appreciate them.

The kids all cheer; they love to go to the radio station.

MIKE. Great; let's go.

ROBERTA. Let's do it.

Lights up on the musicians, who play *"Joy to the World."*

Scene 12

Lights down on the musicians and up on the DJ booth, where all the DJs are gathered.

JON. So what are you guys doing to celebrate Christmas?

ALEX. I'm going to hang out with my family.

JON. That's fun.

JAKE. We're eating way too much.

Everyone laughs.

Big Mike and his family come walking in, and things are tense for just a moment, but then Jon speaks.

JON. Hey, guys, Merry Christmas.

MIKE. Merry Christmas, everyone.

He shakes hands with each DJ; Jon is the last one he comes to.

MIKE. Merry Christmas, Jon.

JON. Merry Christmas, Mike.

MIKE. The family and I wanted to come down and thank you for doing such a wonderful job. The music we've played this year has been pretty amazing, and I've really, really enjoyed it. We thought it was important to have a bit of a celebration with you. So as a little surprise, we made enough money this year to offer a Christmas bonus to each of you.

Mike passes out the envelopes, and each DJ thanks him, clearly overjoyed at the surprise.

MIKE. Well deserved, everyone! And because I know you all love to eat, we brought you all some doughnuts too.

Lots of party chatter occurs while the musicians start to play and lights go out on the stage (up on the musicians).

Scene 13

Lights out on the musicians, and a single spot comes up on Mike, center stage.

MIKE. It's January, a whole new year, and I have a whole new life. Things have been rough in my past, but thanks to some incredible people who were not afraid to speak truth to me, and some incredible music that touched my heart, I have found Jesus. My life is different; my family is happy and healthy, I'm raising my kids in church, and I'm excited for what the future brings. (*He starts to walk off, but quickly turns back.*) Oh, and by the way, KHLY Radio is the newest Christian music station on the market; we're also the best. So Merry Christmas, Arkansas!

Rusty Wall as Big Mike in KHLY Radio

The Treasure of Christmas

This is a really fun story about pirates who are searching for treasure. Their story weaves around that of the Christmas story, but don't worry; it's all in there.

Cast

Mary: a young woman

Joseph: a young man

Gabriel: any age

Angel: any age

Alice: the pirate captain, any age, female

Lefty: the silly (and not-so-smart) pirate, any age

Tobias: a wise pirate (as pirates go), any age

Barnaby: a lovable (but equally ornery) pirate, any age

Innkeeper: any age

Messenger: any age

Townspeople: any age

Sheep: small kids work best

Angels around the manger scene: kids work best

Wise men (3): any age

Shepherds (2): any age

Jeremiah: any age

Scene 1

Lights up on Mary in her room.

Mary stands alone in her bedroom; she is making the bed, folding some blankets, generally straightening things up. Suddenly, a bright light appears, and a voice calls her name.

GABRIEL. Mary.

Mary responds with a reactionary "Yes?" but continues her work, without looking around.

Gabriel becomes visible in the light and speaks again.

GABRIEL. Mary.

MARY. Yes?

This time, she sees the light and the angel, and her "yes" sounds very different than the first one. She begins to recognize that something very supernatural is happening. She doesn't run in fear, though; she senses that it's safe, and while it scares her, she is attentive and listens to what this angel has to say.

GABRIEL. Greetings you, who are highly favored! The Lord is with you. Do not be afraid, Mary; you have found favor with God. You will be with child and give birth to a Son, and you are to give Him the name Jesus. He will be great and will be called the Son of the Most High. The Lord God will give Him the throne of his father David, and he will reign over the house of Jacob forever; His kingdom will never end.

MARY. How can this be? I mean, I am a virgin.

GABRIEL. The Holy Spirit will come upon you, and the power of the Most High will overshadow you. So the holy one to be born will be called the Son of God. Even Elizabeth, your relative, is going to have a child in her old age, and she who was said to be barren is in her sixth month. For nothing, Mary, nothing is impossible with God.

MARY. I am the Lord's servant; may it be as you have said.

The light goes out, and Gabriel disappears.

MARY. I'm going to have a baby? The Son of God will be my baby? What am I going to do? How will I explain this to Joseph? To my parents? Elizabeth! I need to go and see Elizabeth.

Mary runs out of the room, and the lights go out.

Lights up on musicians.

Song: "Mary's Song (Breath of Heaven)."

We see a conversation with Mary and Elizabeth while the song plays; they depart the stage before the song is over, and the stage lights go out, allowing time to set up the carpenter shop.

Musician lights out; carpenter shop lights up.

Scene 2

Joseph stands in his carpenter shop; he is sanding something and muttering to himself.

JOSEPH. I just don't understand it. I thought I did everything right. What possessed Mary to do this to me, to us? I am going to have to cancel the wedding but try to not make a big deal about this. I don't want Mary to be publicly disgraced, either.

Joseph moves over to a comfortable chair in his shop and closes his eyes. He falls asleep. We see an angel, who appears to Joseph in a dream.

ANGEL. Joseph, son of David, do not be afraid to take Mary home as your wife, because what is conceived in her is from the Holy Spirit. She will give birth to a son, and you are to give Him the name Jesus, because He will save his people from their sins. All this has taken place to fulfill what the Lord has said through the prophet: the virgin will be with child and will give birth to a son, and they will call Him Immanuel—which means "God with us."

The angel disappears, and Joseph awakens with a start.

JOSEPH. God with us! God with us! Mary!

Joseph runs off stage, calling for his betrothed.

Lights out on stage while props are moved off.

Lights up on musicians.

At the second verse, lights up center stage (including center aisle) to see Mary and Joseph as described below.

Song: "A Strange Way to Save the World."

We see Mary and Joseph come together during this song. They're committed to fulfill the work the Lord has tasked them and raise the Son of God as best they can. They come back through, and we see Mary's belly is bigger, and then one more time, they come through, with Mary on a donkey, Joseph leading, and parents on stage, waving goodbye.

Lights out.

Scene 3

We see a huge pirate ship (perhaps a video on the screen), and the pirates aboard the ship begin to talk.

Lights up on stage.

Lefty. Ooooo, I be so hungry.

Tobias. Aye, matey. I be hungry too! There ain't no grub to be found on this ship. I think we ate every last rat.

Barnaby. Ugh! Rats! I be sick of fish too.

Tobias. We ain't captured no booty in months; ain't go nottin' to trade; no grub, no grog, no doubloons, no swag. Ain't even got no sprogs to send looking for loot.

Lefty. Ain't even got no lasses; just the ol' wench herself, Alice.

Barnaby. Don't let Alice hear you call her wench; she be sending you to Davy Jones's locker.

Lefty. I ain't a-scared o' no Alice.

Suddenly, the lights go out; we see a strobe light behind a silhouette of Captain Alice with a puff of fog and the sound of thunder.

Alice. Lefty!

Lefty jumps up promptly and looks for a place to hide, scurrying around but unable to get out of sight.

Alice, *appearing on stage.* Lefty, what are you doing? You do nothing but sit around and complain. You and the crew need to get up and catch some fish. We need to charter a new course today.

BARNABY. We be sick of fish, Cap'n! Do you think there be any chance we could go ashore?

LEFTY. Yeah, could we go ashore for at least a little while?

BARNABY. We ain't got nobody out here at sea to pirate no more. Maybe we could find a treasure on land.

TOBIAS. That be a great idea. Let's go lookin' for treasure ashore.

Alice. Well, of all the stupid things ye pirates have ever said, this one ain't so bad! Ashore it is.

The pirates all cheer and yell, "Hooray!" and begin to sing their own pirate song:

ALICE. We're headed for land and looking for loot.

ALL. Yo ho, blow the man down.

LEFTY. I be so hungry I could eat my boot.

ALL. Give me some time to blow the man down.

BARNABY. Don't want no more fish and the rats is all gone.

ALL. Yo ho, blow the man down.

TOBIAS. I never thought I'd be so sick of a song.

ALL. Give me some time to blow the man down.

LEFTY. Who lives in a pineapple under the sea?

ALL. Yo ho, blow the man down.

ALICE. Let's just get to land and see what fortune there be.

ALL. Give me some time to blow the man down.

Lights out to set up the Bethlehem scene.

Scene 4

The people of Bethlehem gather in the town, chattering away in a noisy fashion. The messenger rings a bell to get their attention, and they all fall silent and listen.

MESSENGER. Hear ye, hear ye, people of Bethlehem: A census is being taken, and each man is to register in his own hometown.

The chatter immediately begins again, and the crowd exits the stage; pirates enter through the crowd.

TOBIAS. This place is really crowded. I wonder if we can find a treasure here?

BARNABY. Sure we can; we need to learn how to pick the treasures right off of people.

LEFTY. What are you talking about?

BARNABY. You know, like pick their valuables right off of them without them even noticing.

LEFTY. That's impossible.

BARNABY. I don't know; you could bump into them, apologize, and all the while be snagging their bounty while you distract 'em with talk.

LEFTY. Ain't nobody dumb enough to let that happen to 'em.

ALICE. Really, Lefty? (*Showing him his own coin purse, sword, and even his sandal that she took from him while he listened to Barnaby talk about it.*) You think people is too dumb to let pirates pick their pockets?

All laugh at Lefty, who is totally perplexed as to how Alice got his purse, sword, *and shoe.*

TOBIAS. Okay, let's head to that inn and see if we can get a room. I'm so tired, I could sleep for six days.

ALICE. Good idea, Tobias, let's get us a room and catch some Zs.

Tobias knocks on the door of the inn.

INNKEEPER. Greetings; how may I help you?

TOBIAS. Good afternoon, madam! Would you be so kind as to rent us a room for the night?

INNKEEPER (*Looking at the pirates with complete bewilderment and distaste*). I'm sorry, there's no room in the inn.

BARNABY. No room? Is there another inn?

INNKEEPER. No, I'm sorry. Everything in town is full because of the census. You won't be able to find a room to rent anywhere.

She goes inside and closes the door.

LEFTY. Well, ain't that the pits! What we gonna do now, Cap'n?

ALICE. Toughen up, mates, ye be pirates! Let's hit the road; we'll find a field where we can catch some sleep, and tomorrow, we begin a hunt for treasure.

ALL. Treasure!

All exit.

Aisle lights on

The pirates walk off stage, and Mary and Joseph arrive, coming up the center aisle (on donkey if available).

JOSEPH. Mary, we're here! I know you're so tired; it's been such a long trip. I see a hotel up ahead; let's stop here, and I'll see if I can get us a room.

Joseph stops at a hitching post, and the men there assist with the donkey while he and Mary walk to the inn and knock.

INNKEEPER. Greetings; how may I help you?

JOSEPH. Good afternoon, madam; would you be so kind as to rent us a room for the night? We are here for the census, and my wife is in a motherly way.

INNKEEPER. Oh my, is she ever in a motherly way! I'm so sorry; the inn is full. There are no rooms to rent.

JOSEPH. Okay. Thank you, ma'am; we'll find another inn.

INNKEEPER. No, you don't understand; the town is full. Um ... Oh dear, just hold on a minute. (*She steps back inside the inn and comes out with a stack of blankets.*) Come with me.

They walk across the stage to the barn. She directs Joseph to set a manger aside, while she lays out the blankets and makes a nice bed.

INNKEEPER. It's not much, but it's all we have to offer. I hope you understand, and I hope you are comfortable. I'll bring you out some breakfast in the morning.

MARY. Thank you so much.

JOSEPH. Thank you, ma'am. Thank you. God bless you.

The lights go out on the inn, and a spotlight shines on Mary alone. She begins to look very scared and surprised; she holds her belly and begins to call for Joseph, who has stepped out of the light but is still in the barn.

MARY. Joseph? Joseph? *Joseph!*

Lights out; musician lights on.

Song: "Christ Is Born."

During the song, the lights come up on the manger, and we see an illuminated scene with angels arriving and admiring the King.

Lights out after song for scene change.

Scene 5

Lights up center stage.

The pirates are all asleep in a field; we hear snoring and sleep sounds that become a rhythmic tune, then we hear a noise that wakes Lefty.

LEFTY. What was that?"

TOBIAS, *awakening with a start.* Batten down the hatches.

ALICE. What's going on? What's the trouble?

LEFTY. Something woke me up; I think somebody is coming.

The pirates all awaken and begin to rise.

TOBIAS. Hey, look at that! (*He looks up to the sky as if noticing something surprising.*) Look at that star, or beam of light, or whatever that is. If it's a star, it's the biggest star I've ever seen.

BARNABY. That's huge! What if it's a curse?

TOBIAS. It's not a curse, nimrod! It's a star! We be pirates; we're supposed to understand how to read the stars. Right, Alice?

ALICE. Um, yeah! We're supposed to understand how to read the stars. Right, Lefty?

LEFTY. Yeah, right! We do know how to read the stars; that one says somebody's coming.

Two shepherds appear walking across the stage, and Lefty approaches, attempting his own version of pickpocket.

LEFTY. Ahoy there, mateys! Who goes thar?

Lefty bumps into them and clumsily feels around for anything of value, while the shepherds push him away and Alice encourages him to try again.

SHEPHERD 1. Sir, I'm not at all sure why you need to be so close to my person, but I can tell you that we are shepherds. We have left our flocks to go to the town of David to see the Savior who has been born.

SHEPHERD 2. An angel of the Lord appeared to us and said, "Do not be afraid; I bring you good news of great joy that will be for all the people. Today in the town of David, a Savior has been born to you; he is Christ the Lord. This will be a sign to you; you will find a baby wrapped in cloths and lying in a manger." Then we were surrounded by a sky full of heavenly hosts, praising God and saying, "Glory to God in the highest and on earth, peace to men on whom His favor rests."

LEFTY. You mean to say that angels came to you and told you to go to the town of David?

SHEPHERD 1. Yes, they did.

LEFTY. And you're going? Aren't you scaret?

SHEPHERD 2. At first it was a bit frightening, but even as they spoke the words "Do not be afraid," the fear left me, and I felt peace.

TOBIAS. So you're going to the town of David to see a baby who is the Savior?

SHEPHERD 1. Yes, that's right.

BARNABY. How can a baby be a savior? A baby can't even slash a knife, let alone sword-fight.

PIRATES. Yeah! Yo ho (*laughter*).

SHEPHERD 2. Well, we need to be on our way; safe travels to you.

ALICE. Good day, mates.

The boys make the symbol for crazy when they think the shepherds aren't looking.

ALICE. Did you get any treasure off 'em, Lefty?

LEFTY. They didn't have no treasure on 'em.

BARNABY. Think we oughtta follow 'em and see if they come upon any treasure?

LEFTY. Naw; they be going to see babies, not treasure.

TOBIAS. There be no treasure in a newborn baby.

ALICE. Man ain't worth nothin' till he's old enough to take care of himself and steal enough to share plunder with his mates.

ALL. Yeah! Let's go.

LEFTY. I'm hungry.

TOBIAS. Maybe we'll come upon some rats.

The pirates exit, stage right.

The lights stay on, and when the pirates have cleared the stage, three little lambs crawl across the stage, baaing for their shepherds. They cross the entire stage, and the lights go out.

Scene 6

Lights up.

It's the end of the day, and the pirates have moved on; they are out of the field and crossing some desert land when they come upon a small camel caravan.

ALICE. All right, mates, listen up! Yonder is a group of people coming our way. We don't know what they be doing or where they be going, but if they's after plunder, we gots to find out where it is. What's our mission?

ALL PIRATES. Find treasure!

The men with the camel caravan approach, and Lefty takes the lead.

LEFTY. Good evening, mates! Where ye be headed this fine evening?

WISE MAN 1. Good evening! We are en route to worship the newborn King.

LEFTY. Uh, newborn king, huh? You sure you ain't on a treasure hunt?

WISE MAN 2. It's kind of like a treasure hunt; we have to find the King, and that will take some investigation and searching.

WISE MAN 3. Yes, you're right. A treasure hunt, indeed! He may no longer be in Bethlehem.

WISE MAN 1. That's why we have the star.

WISE MAN 2. Onward!

The wise men chuckle at their funny insight and simply move on.

BARNABY. Did you hear that, Alice? They are on a treasure hunt! Should we follow them?

ALICE. Barnaby, you idiot; they are only looking for a baby. What we gonna do with a baby? I have enough trouble take care of you buccaneers; the last thing I need to add to my daily routine is a baby. No babies.

Pirates walk off stage.

Lights up on musicians.

Song: "We Three Kings."

Lights down.

Scene 7

Lights up on the pirates, all sleepy and propped up against each other to keep from falling over.

TOBIAS. Ya know, I've been thinking about the baby king all these people is going to see.

BARNABY. Yeah? What 'cha thinking about that for?

LEFTY. Yeah, Tobias; what 'cha thinking?

ALICE. Yeah, Tobias; what *are* you thinking about that baby?

She breaks away from the sleeping prop, and the other pirates follow her lead.

TOBIAS. Now calm down. I'm just starting to think that since everyone is looking for this baby, there must be something valuable about it. Also, when you think of kings, what else do you think about?

ALICE. Queens!

BARNABY. Laws.

LEFTY. Yeah, and executions when laws is broken.

They chuckle together and also express a sense of relief that they aren't in trouble with the law at the moment.

ALICE. Guards and thrones.

BARNABY. Crowns.

LEFTY. Royal money.

ALICE. Yeah, money.

BARNABY. Yeah, gold coins and scepters and cups.

ALICE. And jewels and valuables of all kinds.

TOBIAS. Exactly! Mates, we been on the trail of treasure this entire trip and ain't even realized it.

BARNABY. So what do we do now?

ALICE. Mates, get a good night's sleep. Early in the morning, we head to Bethlehem; we'll find that baby.

Song: "The Pirate Song" is sung again as they walk off stage.

ALICE. We're headed for Bethlehem looking for loot.

ALL. Yo ho, blow the man down.

LEFTY. I be so hungry I could eat my boot.

ALL. Give me some time to blow the man down.

BARNABY. Don't want no more fish, and the rats is all gone.

ALL. Yo ho, blow the man down.

TOBIAS. I never thought I'd be so sick of a song.

All. Give me some time to blow the man down.

Lights down as pirates exit stage left; lights up on musicians as Bethlehem is set up.

Lights down after scene is set and music stops.

Scene 8

Lights up on Bethlehem.

Mary and the baby are alone in the barn; she is rocking Him and singing a little lullaby tune when Joseph walks in.

JOSEPH. Mary, I know you're still tired from the birth, and I know you want to go back to Nazareth to see your family, but God has a different plan for us.

MARY. What is it?

JOSEPH. We've been entrusted with the Son of God; it is our responsibility to care for Him and keep Him safe. God will guide us every step of the way, but we have to follow where He leads us. Now He's leading us to Egypt to escape the wrath of angry King Herod. Hope is born, Mary, and Jesus is that hope.

Song: "While You Were Sleeping (Christmas Version)."

While it is sung, we see Mary and Joseph gathering their things to leave for Egypt. Their parents enter from each side of the stage and offer hugs and tears. Mary and Joseph exit down the center aisle, while the parents wave goodbye from the edge of the stage, blowing kisses and comforting each other because part of their family is leaving.

Scene 9

Pirates enter Bethlehem and knock on the door of the inn.

INNKEEPER. Greetings. How may I help you? Oh, it's you again; what are you doing back here?

ALICE. We be looking for the newborn king; we want to worship Him.

LEFTY. Yeah, we want to worship Him. (*They giggle.*)

TOBIAS. We just stopped to get a room for the night.

INNKEEPER. Oh, I see. Well, I'm so sorry, but there is no room in the inn.

BARNABY. What do you mean there's no room in the inn? How can this place be so full all the time?

INNKEEPER. Well, that's easy: since the King was born here, everyone from everywhere is coming to stay here. They want to sleep where the King slept.

LEFTY. Just let us stay in the barn; we be so tired and have some catching up to do tomorrow. We needs to sleep.

ALICE. Yes, the barn will be just fine.

The pirates start to walk toward the barn, but the innkeeper stops them.

INNKEEPER. Wait just a minute; you can't go in there.

LEFTY, *grabbing his sword.* And just why can't we go to the barn?

INNKEEPER. You don't understand; the barn sold out first; that's where the King was born. Jeremiah! Jeremiah!

Jeremiah the stable hand comes out of the barn with a pitchfork in hand and assesses the situation (strange looking pirates and Mrs. Innkeeper hollering for his help).

JEREMIAH. Yes, ma'am?

INNKEEPER. Jeremiah, these, um, these nice, um, these folks here are needing a place to stay, and they seem to think they can just go stay in the barn, even though I've tried to explain that the barn has already been rented, and the inn is full.

JEREMIAH. I see.

LEFTY. Look, ah, Jeremiah, we be weary and need to rest up as to be able to hunt the King at daybreak.

ALICE. Ha, ha, ha. Lefty has quite a way with words; we be looking to *worship* the King. We have to hunt him, I mean find him, in order to be able to worship him, see?

JEREMIAH. I see; why do you want to worship the King? You don't look like Jews, so I'm curious as to why you might want to see the newborn King?

BARNABY. We gonna worship His treasure.

LEFTY. This has been the longest treasure hunt ever.

ALICE, *giving them an elbow to the gut.* Shut up, you scallywags.

JEREMIAH. You are actually right on track if you're treasure hunting.

TOBIAS. We are?

JEREMIAH. Yes; that King who was born here has been the treasure prophesied about for hundreds of years. It's funny that you came looking for financial gain but found eternal wealth instead.

TOBIAS. Eternal wealth? What do you mean?

JEREMIAH. Don't you know? This baby who was born here is the Savior of the world. To find Him is to find salvation, love, peace, joy, eternal hope, and freedom. Money has no purpose in heaven. Jesus is the provider of all things. Knowing Jesus is the greatest treasure in the world.

LEFTY. Arr … How do we get that treasure?

BARNABY. Arr … Where do we find it?

JEREMIAH. "Arr" is exactly how you find it.

ALICE. Arr … what?

1. JEREMIAH. Just a little pun. But seriously, think of the four Arrs: Arr #1: Recognize the treasure when you see it.
   ALICE. Arr-recognize it.
   JEREMIAH. It's not in a wooden treasure chest or a gold coin. Jesus is the treasure. He is the way, the truth, and the life, and no one will come to the Father but through Him. You're very right when you think that the King has a treasure; Jesus has the most valuable treasure of them all to share with you.
2. JEREMIAH. Arr #2: Reach for the treasure.
   TOBIAS. Arr-reach for it.
   JEREMIAH. In order to reach for it, you have to know where to find it and then claim it for your own. Jesus can be found right where you are. You don't have to travel the globe or sleep where He slept or meet Him in person. He will meet you right where you are, even on your ship. Admit that you're a sinful person (let's face it, we all are). Believe that Jesus is the perfect Son of God. Confess your sins to Him, and claim Him as your Savior and King.

3. JEREMIAH. Arr #3: Respect the treasure.
   BARNABY. Arr-respect it.
   JEREMIAH. This treasure is really a gift. You don't have to steal it or hide it for fear that someone will take it from you. Let the whole world know that Jesus saves and that you are the wealthiest pirates in the world because you have the treasure of Jesus in your hearts.
4. JEREMIAH. Finally, Arr #4: Rejoice in the treasure.
   LEFTY. Arr-rejoice in it.
   JEREMIAH. Nothing in the world, not gold, silver, money, food, friendships, family, or even pirating will bring you joy like the joy of knowing Jesus. Celebrate it. Praise His name. Share His joy, and feel the love that only Jesus can bring.

LEFTY. So the baby is the treasure?

JEREMIAH. Yes.

BARNABY. And we don't have to steal it to have it?

JEREMIAH. That's right; the treasure is a gift. It's free.

LEFTY. All we have to do is ask?

TOBIAS. And believe?

JEREMIAH. That's right. Admit you're a sinner, believe that Jesus is the Son of God, confess your sins to Him, and claim Him as your Savior; that's the action. The treasure is salvation and eternal life.

ALICE. I ain't never heard of no treasure that good; you don't even need a map to find it? Arr!

LEFTY. Four arrs!

The pirates laugh and shake hands with Jeremiah, who then steps forward and speaks directly to the crowd. As he does, the cast lines up for curtain call; music starts.

JEREMIAH. Ladies and gentlemen, we thank you for coming to our play tonight, and we pray this Christmas season, you and your family find the Arrs in the message of His birth. May God bless you.

The Christmas Day

This is probably the most personal play a church can do. It's an opportunity for church members to give a little testimony or tell a true story about themselves. The premise is this: If you could have been present when Jesus was born, what gift would you have brought? Some would bring a song, a poem, or a story; others, a gift of some kind. Members should explain why their gifts have meaning. This is a fun and a personal Christmas program that invites the community to come and see what you're really all about. Included are a couple of the stories that were written for some of the boys in the church. They chose to do their presentations in groups of two, and the script was written for them. We used a screen to show some images behind the presenters. Some of our presentations were very personal, with members speaking of childhood trauma or growing up in abuse and explaining how grateful they are for the redemptive grace of Jesus. Others were mere reflections of the joy that the people feel knowing why Jesus came to earth on Christmas. The director has to help people with their selections and order the presentations in a fashion that creates an interesting flow. Choose a narrator who can add some fill-in between presenters, if necessary.

NARRATOR. Welcome to our church; this church is our home. It's where we gather as a family in Christ to pay extra special attention to our King, our Lord and Savior, Jesus Christ. Christmastime at our church is an especially important time. Christmas is the celebration of the earthly birthday of Jesus. It's so very amazing to think He came to this earth to be with us, walk with us, talk with us, serve us, teach us, love us, and die for us. What a very amazing gift we received that very first Christmas.

The manger scene is a classic Christmas symbol, full of meaning to Christians across the world. For some people, it is simply a Christmas decoration, a beautiful picture of what they think is just a beautiful story of love, but a story they may not believe to be true. For us, it's different. The manger scene is everything we believe to be true. Our faith, our hope, our entire lives are built upon the truth that Jesus Christ, born on this day two thousand years ago, was the Son of God who came to earth to die for our sins, thus allowing us to enter heaven one day when we pass from this earth. The really good news is that He remains the Son of God, reigning in heaven at the right hand of the Father, interceding on our behalf.

You know, the interesting thing about the manger scene (Mary, Joseph, and baby Jesus) is that it didn't remain just a manger scene for long. What we now call the nativity scene (all the visitors present at the manger) came to life as people quickly came to visit the newborn baby and welcome Him to the world. Do you think those people really knew who Jesus was? Did they realize that He had come to earth to serve as the sacrifice for our sins? I don't know if they did or not. They knew there was a huge star in the sky, and they felt compelled to follow it. They knew something big was happening because the angels came to see them and tell them to go and see the newborn King. But did they really understand the history that was being made? Did they recognize that they would be part of the story we would tell for thousands of years to come? I doubt they really understood all of that. Let's say you could go back to the day that Christ was born; knowing what you know now.

If you woke up on Christmas morning and an angel told you to follow the star, what would you say when you arrived to see the infant King? Let's see what happens when the people of Calvary Missionary Baptist Church get that opportunity.

Lucas and Julian: A Selfie with the King

JULIAN. There He is, look! I can hardly believe we found Him.

LUCAS. Hi, Jesus; you may not know us now, but you will one day. I'm Lucas.

JULIAN. And I'm Julian; we have learned all about you. You are going to live a really full life.

LUCAS. Yeah, when people find out what kind of incredible power you have, they will want to be close to you. People will come from all over just to see you; they will wait in line just to touch you.

JULIAN. You'll be famous.

LUCAS. Yeah, famous. But you won't have a lot of money or anything.

JULIAN. And you won't be on television; there won't be any television when you're here.

LUCAS. You won't be liked by everybody either. Some people will be really mean to you.

JULIAN. Some people are just bullies. We've had to face bullies before too, Jesus. Having good friends helps; you'll have some really good friends in your time.

LUCAS. Yes, you'll have twelve good friends, but even some of them won't always have your back. But don't worry, Jesus. We love you.

JULIAN. Yeah! We love you a lot. Thank you for everything you will do for us.

LUCAS. Yeah, thanks! Hey, Jesus, would it be okay if …

They pull out a cell phone, and the stage goes black; a selfie of Lucas and Julian with baby Jesus appears on the screen.

Justin and Dayton: An Autograph from the King

The boys approach the front of stage slowly, elbowing each other as if to get the other to go first.

DAYTON. Who else could it be?

JUSTIN. Well, I don't know.

DAYTON. Come on, let's get closer. Hi, baby Jesus. We wanted to come and meet you.

JUSTIN. To welcome you to the world. We're glad you're here.

DAYTON. Really glad.

JUSTIN. We are in the third grade this year, Jesus. Thank you for helping us in school.

DAYTON. Thank you for helping us in football.

JUSTIN. Yeah! And thank you for our families.

DAYTON. For my sister.

JUSTIN. And my sister and brothers; I have two brothers, and I don't always love them like I should, but I try to. I know you want us to love everybody.

DAYTON. Our Sunday school teacher always says we are supposed to love God and love people. We always try to be nice and show love to people, just like you say we should.

JUSTIN. One time, my brother broke my favorite game character. I was so mad at him that I said I would never talk to him again. But I did, and eventually, I started to like him again, but it took a while. I had to learn that You love me even when I don't always act nice. So I needed to love my brothers and my sister when I think they don't act nice. Anyway, I just wanted to say thanks for helping me learn how to be nice even when I don't feel like it.

DAYTON. Thank you, Jesus, for everything. I love You with my whole heart. We brought You a present; it's a toy. We hope You like it.

They boys set a wrapped gift at the edge of the stage.

JUSTIN. Bye, baby Jesus.

DAYTON. Oh, um, Jesus?

Dayton shows the baby his football, and the lights go out. A picture of the football with a baby footprint on it shows on the screen.

These are two small examples of things you can help your kids do to show their love for Jesus. The adults can bring their own unique stories, poems, songs, or gifts that represent them and how they relate to Jesus as their Savior. The play can be as long or as short as you want it to be, depending on how many people want to join in. One man sang the song "If That Don't Make You Want to Go" because it tied in so nicely with the narrator summary.

If That Don't Make You Want to Go

CHARLIE. It's an honor to be present on the first Christmas Day; to see the newborn King is overwhelming and joyous. I didn't bring a gift. I'm still working on my gift. I know that every day, I am working to build treasure in heaven. I'm working to earn more jewels for the crown that one day I'll give You, King Jesus. I'll lay it at Your feet and spend my eternity praising You. I'm a blessed man to be surrounded by people who know and love You. I'm a blessed man to live in a country that is founded on Your principles and laws. I'm a blessed man to know You personally. It's an honor to serve You. Seeing You today is thrilling; seeing You in heaven will be more than I could possibly ever imagine.

Song: "If That Don't Make You Want to Go."

NARRATOR. Well, there you have it; when today's Christians come face-to-face with their King of Kings on His birthday, wow, oh wow! What a wonderful reunion of love. To think that our King was willing to come to earth as an infant, completely vulnerable and at the mercy of young parents to raise Him; how amazing! We know that God was ever present in that baby, and you know what else we know? When we accept Jesus as our Savior and King, we are heirs to the kingdom of God, joint heirs with Jesus. It's not really possible for us to travel back in time and see Jesus when He was here on this earth. But we will see Him one day. One day, we will have the opportunity to give Him the gift we've prepared for Him. We will lay our crown at His feet. Where does that crown come from? Good question; you are given a crown by God when you believe on Him, admit that He died on the cross for your sins, and accept Him as your Savior. Every moment of every day from that point forward, you are adorning your crown. When you read your Bible and pray (your communication with God), when you serve God by serving others, and when you live with kindness and love and not out of selfish desires, these things adorn the crown you will one day give Jesus. Be thinking about the gift you will give the King. Will it be all you intend for it to be? You can't buy it, you can't borrow it, and you can't make it something it's not. It will be a tangible picture of your love and commitment to your King. I know I can hardly wait for *the* Christmas Day.

Tricks of the Trade

Start Early

If you're doing a Christmas play, try to select the play by the end of September so you can cast the parts and pass the script out to everyone in a timely fashion. Most church members cannot attend extra nights of the week to have play practice, so you typically have to build it into the church routine those few months before Christmas. Try replacing Wednesday night or Sunday night services with play practice. This can mean as few as eight practices before a production, so you may need an afternoon practice the day of (or the day before) the play, just to be sure everyone is fresh the day of the performance.

Pick the Characters

Use your best judgment to cast parts rather than holding auditions. Most of the time, when you've selected a play and read through it, you have a vision for what you want it to be and who could play the parts. Holding auditions is simply a competition for parts, and this can cause a great deal of hurt feelings for members who all want the same part or are a bit afraid of the stage. People are often much more willing to help if you simply ask them to do something specific; it's theirs, they own it, and they will do their best with it. Don't forget to pick people for all the extra things you need. Who will run the lights? Who will move the scene changes on the stage? Who will control the microphones (if you're lucky enough to have them)?

Be Organized

Write out the lighting cues you want and when you want them, so the people controlling the lights have something to follow.

Write out a list of the props and write the movement of the props on and off the stage into the script you provide the cast. Each cast member needs to have a clear understanding of everything they need to do (e.g., enter stage left with flowers and suitcase, exit stage right with jacket, etc.).

Write out the scene changes and identify who moves what pieces of the set.

As the play practices progress and you discover things that work well, write them down and then write them into the direction sheets you provide for the cast. Tape them up backstage in a variety of places so the cast all has a go-to place to see what scene is next and what they need to do next. On the night of the actual play, everyone will be nervous. These organizing sheets are so helpful.

Practice everything from the welcome to the curtain call, including turning the house lights off and on. These little things can really cause a disaster if you aren't prepared for them.

Be Encouraging

Many people have never been on stage before. Learning to do it can be fun, but it can also be stressful. Be encouraging and make public note of it when someone does a great job. You do have to be careful to not always compliment the same people and leave others without any positive feedback at all. Try to create a nurturing environment that inspires people to do a good job. Who learned the most lines? Who remembered all their cues? Who was most improved over last practice? Who had a great idea to make a scene better? Praise those achievements and cheer for each other. Sometimes, you'll find you're laughing at each other too because it can really be funny. Be sure that the person receiving the laughter is receiving it in the right way, not as a personal attack. If you can keep everyone in the right spirit, this will be the most fun thing your church ever does.

Find Your Experts

As you do more plays, you'll discover who is most comfortable on stage and who is more effective behind the scenes. Some people prefer to help make sure everything goes off without a hitch instead of portraying a character. These people are great stage ninjas. They dress in all black and change the scenes in the dark, ensuring everything is set up where it is supposed to be for the actors. Some like to build set pieces; others paint the sets so they look realistic. Some love to do costumes, others make the program for the night of the performance, and others greet the audience the night of the play. You also need someone to run the lights. (For some churches, this is only shutting off the lights over the audience and leaving on the lights over the stage. If those are the only theater lights you have, that's okay.).

Advertise

You need to advertise. To invest the time and energy it takes to do a play and not have a crowd come to see it is hugely disappointing and discouraging for your entire congregation. Most newspapers, radio stations, and local cable channels offer free advertising in their community calendars. Use social media to advertise and hype up the performance to increase interest. Facebook is a great format for this. Take pictures at practices and post them. Write a little teaser about the play and encourage people to come and see what happens. Coordinate with community events. If your town has a local Christmas parade, have the cast walk the parade in costume and pass out invitations. Post flyers in all of the local restaurants and shops. Ask the local newspaper editor to come to a practice and do a story about the play, encouraging people to come the night of the performance. Getting the community excited gets the cast and crew excited, and they work hard to ensure it's a great show.

Share Jesus

Remember that doing these plays is a ministry, a service to our Lord and Savior Jesus Christ. This is a format churches can use to reach people who may otherwise never step foot into a church or hear the Word of God. Each practice should start with a prayer, and every attitude on and off stage should be focused on using this opportunity to share the love of Jesus. There shouldn't be egos on stage, only servants of the Lord. Satan will stress you and try you and do everything in his power to cause you to believe the production will fail. Just remember that the harder he works to ruin the event, the bigger the impact the effort will have if you press on toward the prize and share this ministry with your community.

May God bless you as you step into this fun and exciting ministry.

Musicians Andy, Rachelle, Charlie, Rodger and David

Music Credits

4Him. *Christmas, the Season of Love.* Capitol 84418-2187-2, 1993, compact disc. Harris, Mark, Don Koch, and Dave Clark. *Strange Way to Save the World.*

Alma Gluck and Paul Reimas. *Stille Nacht, Heilige Nacht.* Victor 87284, B-20683/2 Sept 19, 1917, 10". Franz, Gruber. *Silent Night.* 1818.

Amy Grant. *A Christmas Album.* Myrrh, Reunion Records, 1983, compact disc and vinyl promo. Eaton, Chris. *O Little Town.* 1982.

Amy Grant. *Home for Christmas.* Sparrow Records, 1992, compact disc. *Breath of Heaven (Mary's Song).*

BarlowGirl. *Home for Christmas.* Fervent Records, 2008, compact disc and digital download. Originally released Sept 23, 2008. Barlow, Alyssa, Lauren Barlow, and Rebecca Barlow. *Hallelujah Light Has Come.*

Casting Crowns. *Peace on Earth.* Reunion 5264, 2008, compact disc and digital download. Hall, John Mark. *While You Were Sleeping (Christmas Version).*

Edison Male Quartette. *Jingle Bells.* First recording, 1898, Edison cylinder. Pierpont, James. *Jingle Bells.* 1850.

Harry Simeone Chorale. *Do You Hear What I Hear?* Mercury-72065, 1962, vinyl 7", 45RPM Promo. Originally released Dec 7, 1962. Regney, Noel, and Gloria Shayne Baker.

Isaac Watts. *The Psalms of David: Initiated in the Language of the New Testament, and Applied to the Christian State of Worship.* London, 1719. Watts, Isaac and Handel, George Fridenic. *Joy to the World.* 1719

John Henry Hopkins Jr. *Carols, Hymns & Songs.* 1862. Hopkins, John Henry Jr. *We Three Kings.* 1857.

Josh Turner and Missy Robertson. *Duck the Halls.* Capitol Records Nashville, EMI Records Nashville, B0019025-02, 2013, compact disc. Turner, Josh. *Why I Love Christmas.* 2013.

Mark Harris. *Christmas Is.* Columbia/Sony Music Distribution, 2009, compact disc. Harris, Mark. *The Caroler's Song/Angles We Have Heard on High.* 2009.

Patty, and Mildred J. Hill. *Songs for the Kindergarten.* Clayton F. Summy OCoLC-894106125, OCLC-57148282, 1896. *Happy Birthday.* 1893.

Point of Grace. *A Christmas Story.* Word Records, 1999, compact disc. Borders, Jeff, Gayla Borders, and Lowell Alexander. *One King.* 1998.

Ramsey Murray and Kirkpatrick, William J. "Away In A Manger." 1887 and 1895.

The Carpenters. *Christmas Portrait.* A&M SP-4726; 3947262, Aug 1, 1993, vinyl/cassette/8-track/compact disc. Dominico Barolucci and Ray Charles. *Christ Is Born.*

The Collingsworth Family. *Part of the Family.* Stowtown Records, 2011, compact disc. *Joy Unspeakable.*"

The Collingsworth Family. *Part of the Family.* Stowtown Records, 2011, compact disc. Newell, William, and Daniel Towner. *At Calvary.* 1895.

The Collingsworth Family. *Part of the Family.* Stowtown Records, 2011, compact disc. *Jesus Is All I Need.*

The Collingsworth Family. *Part of the Family*. Stowtown Records, 2011, compact disc. *Nothing's Worrying Me.*

The Collingsworth Family. *Part of the Family*. Stowtown Records, 2011, compact disc. *I Pray.*

The Collingsworth Family. *Part of the Family*. Stowtown Records, 2011, compact disc. *Just Another Rainy Day.*

The Collingsworth Family. *Part of the Family*. Stowtown Records, 2011, compact disc. *The Resurrection Morn.*

The Isaacs. *Heroes*. EMI CMG 0617884251451, 2004, cassette/compact disc/digital download. Gaither, Bill, and Gloria. *If That Don't Make You Want to Go.*

The Trapp Family Singers. *Christmas with the Trapp Family Singers*. Decca Records, 1941, Vinyl 7", 45RPM. Originally released in 1941. Davis, Katherine Kennicot. *The Little Drummer Boy.*

About the Author

Rodg, Holly and Lucas standing

Holly Langster is a fifteen-year resident of Heber Springs, Arkansas, where she resides with her husband, Rodger, and her son, Lucas. Holly has been involved in drama since high school, where she participated in several high school plays. After high school, her favorite pastime became community theater. Today using all the helpful things she learned from her directors over the years, Holly brings drama to her local church and community.

Printed in the United States
By Bookmasters